Handling Hot Potatoes
Healing Broken Hearts

With best wishes.

Victor Maxwell

Rom 8:31.

Handling Hot Potatoes
Healing Broken Hearts

VICTOR MAXWELL

AMBASSADOR

Belfast Northern Ireland Greenville South Carolina

Handling Hot Potatoes - Healing Broken Hearts
© Copyright 2000 Victor Maxwell

ISBN 1 84030 077 9

Ambassador Publications
a division of
Ambassador Productions Ltd.
Providence House
Ardenlee Street,
Belfast,
BT6 8QJ
Northern Ireland
www.ambassador-productions.com

Emerald House
427 Wade Hampton Blvd.
Greenville
SC 29609, USA
www.emeraldhouse.com

Introduction

CHRISTIANS ARE OFTEN BLAMED FOR BEING IMPRACTICAL AND UNREALISTIC. SOMETIMES THEY ARE VIEWED AS BEING TOO selective and only focusing on the positive and simple aspects of life. Pastors are accused of being quick to major on the prospect of a glorious heaven but bury their heads when it comes to the gory pains of this life.

Perhaps these criticisms are justified by the attitude of some Christians who choose to ignore the suffering and problems ordinary people face in what is commonly called "the real world." However, any honest reader of the Scriptures must admit that the Bible is not silent on human hurt. Furthermore, the same Scriptures disclose that godly people of all generations have not been immune to the practical difficulties and painful dilemmas that ordinary people face today. Problems and pain are something we all have in common. Christians bleed, cry and hurt like other people. Our faith in Jesus Christ does not insulate us from afflictions and heartache.

In this book I have attempted to look at some of the agonizing and distressing issues people face today.

Rebellion in the heart of Africa threatens missionaries,
A bomb tragedy in Omagh kills twenty-nine people.
An earthquake in Japan destroys the heart of Kobe.
A rape in England reveals the horror of a home.
Suicide afflicts young and old.
Homosexuality has become an acceptable lifestyle.
Substance abuse is on the increase.
Bad news from the doctor is frightening.
Empty arms and imperfect infants break hearts.

These are the painful problems I have faced eyeball to eyeball in this book.

I have met and interviewed people who have come through very hurtful experiences and have endeavoured to give an accurate account of their story. Many of them still wrestle with unanswered questions and shed tears because of their painful past. I thank them most sincerely for their kind co-operation. To all of them I have tried to apply the Scriptures of truth and comfort to their situations, both while present in their company and also in this book.

With each case history I have endeavoured to avoid the pitfall of offering trite and simplistic answers to involved and complex questions and problems. Where necessary I have indicated that the names of people and places have been changed to protect the identity of individuals. The interviews, investigations and application of the Scriptures to each case are not exhaustive. This is an honest attempt to face some difficulties head on and to help and encourage from the Scriptures those who carry aching hearts.

As Christians we have no power over things that happen to us. However, we do have the power of God within us to cope with and overcome the difficulties we may encounter.

Before reading this book I suggest that it will be of benefit for any who face any difficulty in life to read from the best Book – the Holy Scriptures, in Psalms 34 and 37.

Victor Maxwell

Contents

Chapter one

Daylight Danger

THE EERIE DARKNESS SEEMED TO FOLD ITS CLAMMY LAYERS AROUND MAUD AS SHE LAY AWAKE ON HER SINGLE BED IN THE middle of the tropical night. Beads of perspiration on her brow edged to meet each other and merged into twisting riblets of sweat which ran through her hair and unto the uncomfortable pillow. The bedroom's thick brick walls did not deaden the piercing whine which sounded from crickets and beetles or the deep croak of seemingly hundreds of frogs in the surrounding jungle. The cacophony of jungle noises only accentuated the tension Maud felt as her heart pounded with a heavy and rhythmic beat like jungle drums.

Maud knew that the noises inside the house came from either the scurrying of rodents in the rafters or from her colleague Margaret who was in the adjoining room. Margaret Coleman was a former colleague of Maud in Africa, and she had returned to Congo for a six week visit. Maud was encouraged to know that Margaret was planning to spend some time with her at the mission station.

The gabble of the drunken soldiers who occupied the mission compound could also be clearly heard echoing in the night . Maud prayed for protection for herself and for Margaret from the evil intent of their would-be captors. Her busy mind ran over the events of the previous twenty-four hour period, and she shuddered to think of what might have been. Her thoughts soon mingled with thanksgiving for God's good hand upon her and with prayers for what the dawn of the new day might hold.

It seemed strange that Maud's troubled heart and tense mind alternated with waves of peace which flooded her being as she recalled the promises God had given to her when she first left home to serve the Lord in the heart of Africa. She had proved those promises to be sure and dependable since she arrived in the Republic of the Congo in 1968. Much had happened since that time. Congo was known as Zaire from 1971 through to 1997. Now she would need to prove them again in the Democratic Republic of the Congo.

The massacres and genocide that accompanied the conflict between the Hutu and Tutsi tribes in Rwanda, where over half a million people had lost their lives, had slowly spilled over the border into neighbouring Congo as thousands of refugees fled to escape the Rwandan killings. The Congo was already a troubled country whose precarious economy had given rise to much civil unrest. In 1996 following the Rwandan conflict General Laurent Kabila, a seasoned fighter in Congo, led an army of volunteer soldiers assisted by Rwanda and Uganda to overthrow President Mobutu Sese Seko who had ruled Congo for more than thirty-two years.

As the conflict spread east there was much killing and looting by both sides in the bloody and brutal war. Soon it became unsafe and unwise for missionaries serving God in isolated jungle areas to remain at their mission stations. Many were evacuated to neighbouring Kenya. Others were repatriated to their native lands. Maud Kells was forced to return to her home in Cookstown, Northern Ireland.

This was not the first evacuation for Maud. She had served as a Worldwide Evangelization for Christ (WEC) missionary nurse in Congo for over thirty years and had dedicated her nursing skills to bring relief from suffering to some of the Congo's remote and needy people. Several times she and her fellow missionaries had been given only twenty-four hours notice to leave their mission station with no more than five kilos of baggage. Many times in their absence their possessions had been looted or confiscated, their houses, hospital and clinic plundered. On one occasion Maud had her valuable Land Rover seized by the invading soldiers and had to suffer the loss of the vehicle.

After the defeat and exile of President Mobutu, General Laurent Kabila and his forces seized power in the country. What was formerly known as Zaire became the Democratic Republic of the Congo under Kabila. A green light was given to foreign missionaries who were anxious to return to the land and people they loved and served. With the assurance of her praying partners behind her and her confidence in the promises and providence of Almighty God, Maud returned to Congo in April 1998.

On Easter Sunday her flights took her from Belfast to Amsterdam and then on by KLM jet to Nairobi in Kenya where she was joined by Margaret Coleman on Easter Monday. Early on Tuesday morning they boarded a Samaritan's Purse aircraft in Nairobi and flew high over the frontiers of Kenya, Uganda and Congo making a stop in Entebbe before arriving in Kisangani.

After passing through the Emigration procedures at Kissangani Maud tried to persuade the missionary pilot that instead of her and Margaret remaining in Kissangani as was originally planned, he extend his flight to Mulita which was their final destination. This would save a lot of time and inconvenience for the two lady missionaries. The pilot agreed to their request.

The single engine plane climbed into the sky above Kisangani early that April morning. As the airplane steadily followed its course Maud looked down on the green forest below which seemed to roll on endlessly like an emerald carpet. Her thoughts began to wander as she thought of this land she had adopted as her home. Under the canopy of these forests the once ecological paradise, which was extremely rich in natural resources, was now marred by long arteries of red clay where dirt roads tore up the jungle and large mounds of earth indicated the exploration of mineral mines.   These scars on the topography of the landscape were analogous to the wounds and disfigurement that civil unrest was again bringing to these equatorial regions.   Anarchy was spreading like a virulent infection out of control.   It was tearing the Congo apart and robbing the country of its great potential.

Maud and her missionary colleagues had come to these regions to bring the message of the gospel to thousands of forest dwellers whose lives were marred and ruined by superstition and sin.   Since 1913 when C. T. Studd, the famous cricketer and missionary pioneer, sailed to the heart of Africa a long succession of missionaries had dedicated their lives to reaching these people for the cause of Jesus Christ. They had built hospitals, leprosaria, schools, colleges and had seen the Church of Jesus Christ grow from the early pioneer work in primitive conditions to experience outpourings of revival and great blessing. The price had been high but these missionaries followed the principle expressed by the founder of WEC, "If Jesus Christ be God and died for me, then no sacrifice can be too great for me to make for Him."

At last the small aircraft was nearing Mulita and she was happy to be going back to the work and believers she loved, but she wondered how things would be on her arrival. Would the hospital still be operating? Would the Bible School still be functioning? Who will have cared for the leprosy patients? Would the workers still be at their posts? These are only a few of the questions that had occupied Maud's thoughts and also had been the burden of her prayers during her forced absence from Mulita.

After an hour in the air the pilot circled his plane over the mission station to indicate to those on the compound that the lady missionaries were arriving. The sight of the familiar mud buildings painted white and covered in reflective aluminum roofs that gleamed in the early sunlight excited Maud and Margaret. The pilot lined his plane up for landing on the grass air-strip etched out of the forest. Soon the wheels touched down, and the plane rumbled to a stop where a large crowd of African friends was congregated to welcome the missionaries back.

When they disembarked from the plane and after a few initial greetings to familiar friends, Maud and Margaret were startled to find that a group of young soldiers was in control of the mission station. The soldiers were brash and brazen as they surrounded the plane and barked orders to the new arrivals. The commanding officer impounded the plane and told the pilot that because his papers were not in order and soon all private air-strips would be closed, he must remain at Mulita.

Maud and Margaret refused to leave the air-strip while the controversy continued about the plane. At first the pilot tried to reason with the officer that he needed to return to his family. The officer would have none of it and became quite aggressive towards the pilot. The stand-off between the missionaries and the officer continued for almost two hours in the hot sun. During this time many bulletin prayers were made to heaven.

The pilot went to the cockpit of the plane to radio his wife back at their base and inform her he was being detained in Mulita. Unexpectedly the army commander intervened and gave the pilot permission to leave. God answered prayer and finally the plane was released. The pilot wasted no time in speeding down the air-strip and climbing into the sky and out of a delicate and volatile atmosphere below.

Once the Samaritan's Purse plane was released the missionaries began to make their way to the mission houses. Just then a messenger came running asking Maud to go to the maternity unit urgently as an expectant mother was in great distress. As Maud rushed to the hospital compound she discovered that the band of young soldiers were billeted throughout the hospital and had taken over the guest house. With a young mother in agony at the unit there was no time to remonstrate about the action of the soldiers.

The lady in the maternity unit was suffering because she was unable to deliver her baby. As Maud scrubbed up she learned that the expectant mother's anguish was made even worse by the fact that her other child had just died from malnutrition. Maud forgot about the recent stress at the airstrip and prayed for strength, grace and wisdom from heaven to help in the confinement of this lady. For the next hour and a half Maud and the midwives sweated and prayed as they worked with the mother. Finally, Maud was able to deliver the baby by the use of forceps.

The arrival of the newborn not only brought relief to the mother and all concerned but caused Maud to lift her heart in gratitude to God. If Maud had not arrived at that precise time then most certainly the baby would have died and the mother's life would have been in grave danger. The African midwives added to Maud's thanksgiving when they exclaimed, "Mademoiselle, while you were away there were no difficult deliveries. Now that you have just returned this lady arrived. God sent you to us for this very hour."

The comment confirmed to Maud that God had brought her to the right place at the right time even though things at the mission station did not seem favourable.

With the emergency at the maternity unit taken care of Maud made her way back through the mission compound toward her house. The soldiers were waiting for her. They made her and Margaret unpack all the baggage they had brought on the plane. When the soldiers had searched through all their belongings they turned their attention to the nine barrels of equipment that Maud had shipped from United Kingdom. Even though Maud assured them that the baggage had been cleared at customs they still ordered her to open the barrels one by one. Meticulously they went through the contents of the barrels. It was evident they were searching for arms but obviously none was found.

Young gun-touting boys in uniform had set up a barricade on the road that passed by the mission station. All who passed by were ordered to stop and show what goods they carried. Any who failed to stop were brutally beaten near to the mission house. At times the scenes were too gruesome to look on. Many of the young men in uniform seemed to be crazed by drugs or drink. Over the course of the next few weeks five people were bludgeoned to death, and one of the bodies was thrown into a nearby stream.

By the time the inspection of the barrels was completed it was nearly dark. The mission house had not been lived in for two years. The air inside the house was damp and stale. What furniture was left in the house was covered in an ample deposit of dust and rodent droppings. Little could be done to clean or reorganize the house with the approach of nightfall. However, after consuming some African food and removing new bed sheets from the baggage, the two girls fixed their bedrooms to try to catch some sleep.

Before retiring for the evening Maud and Margaret earnestly prayed. They thanked God for His protection in the midst of danger, for the real peace they enjoyed in their hearts in spite of the adverse circumstances and for the wisdom given to help in the delivery of the newborn baby at the maternity unit. There was so much to pray about and thank God for. However, they were weary from all the happenings of the long and eventful day, so they turned in for the night.

Sleep did not come easily that night. Maud thought of the threats made on the pilot. She also mused on the irony of the dramatic arrival of the newborn baby at the maternity unit contrasted against the senseless and barbaric killing of local villagers nearby. Eventually Maud drifted into semi-consciousness and then into a deep sleep.

The singing of the birds on the trees outside and the bright sunlight streaming into the musty bedroom woke Maud out of her sleep at 5.30 a.m.. Busy days lay ahead for her and Margaret and they wasted no time getting started. The next few weeks were taken up with sorting out the mission house, reorganizing the hospital and attending to a steady stream of out-patients who arrived early each day. During the next two weeks three more forceps deliveries were necessary at the maternity unit, and besides these, the leprosy patients were in great need of attention.

The presence of so many soldiers billeted in the hospital made nursing care very difficult. After Maud engaged in much talking and negotiation a three-hour meeting was convened with all the local chiefs in the area. At this meeting it was decided to order the local population to build mud houses to accommodate the young men in uniform.

At first the troops were reluctant to move out from the comfort of the hospital but eventually they were persuaded to transfer to these newly constructed, simple buildings.

The pharmacy needed to be reorganized; new mattresses were made for the hospital; mission buildings were repaired and new premises were built for the increased number of leprosy patients. It was an extremely busy time for every one, but Maud was enjoying being back in her familiar surroundings with many people she had grown to love

Added to the pressure of the medical work there were serious problems in the church. Some of the church leaders had succumbed to immorality, and there was a division amongst the believers in the measure of discipline that should be exercised on these disgraced leaders. Bible School students who had come from many other parts of the Congo had missed the presence of the missionaries. Now that the two ladies had returned the students felt that their Bible training programme should be given urgent attention. Many hours were spent counselling students, advising leaders and encouraging believers.

After several weeks Margaret left Mulita to return home to England. The news reports coming in from other parts of the Congo were not good. Political tension was high as the Tutsi-led government of Rwanda reacted against President Kabila's campaign to repatriate all Rwandan refugees back to their native country. Another scourge of terror threatened as followers of former President Mobutu joined forces with the Tutsi in Rwanda to fight against Kabila's Hutu-backed regime. Many of these soldiers were only thirteen and fourteen-year-old boys. The fractured infrastructure of the country sent inflation spiralling out of control. Petrol and everyday essentials were beyond the reach of many and the black market thrived in the vacuum.

There were reports of terrible atrocities and rumours ran wild of what was going to be the outcome. However, Maud had heard a lot of these sort of reports before and she felt secure amongst those whom she knew in Mulita.

Just when life seemed to be returning to normal, communication came from the WEC headquarters in far-off Isiro summoning the missionaries for a Field Conference at the beginning of August. Normally Field Conferences are convened in March or April, but because of the unrest and disruption experienced in the previous year it was felt that there should be a meeting of the missionaries and church leaders much earlier.

Unfortunately the Government had ordered the closure of all small private airstrips. This prevented Maud and her friends flying out of Mulita. On Tuesday, July 21, 1998, because of the government order, Maud and two pastors from the Mulita church had to cycle on the mud road for three hours in the hot sun to reach the airfield at neigbouring Punia. There they waited the arrival of the Missionary Aviation Fellowship plane which was bringing in a consignment of books, medicines and equipment for the hospital. Sixteen workmen had accompanied Maud and her fellow passengers the twenty-two miles to the airfield. The men were employed to carry the boxes of equipment back to Mulita.

In the shade of the trees at the airfield the passengers and work group patiently waited for several hours, but the plane did not arrive. Word finally came through to say that the weather was bad and the plane could not make the journey. The same procedure of going to the airport early was followed for the next three days, but on each occasion the flight was cancelled because of bad weather. However, Maud was not frustrated for the extra days in Mulita allowed her to spend more time ironing out some problems at the hospital.

On Friday morning a tropical thunder storm awakened Maud just before dawn. The heavy downpour indicated that there was little likelihood that the plane would arrive on such a day. During prayer time at 6:30 a.m. Maud claimed Proverbs 3:5,6. "Trust in the Lord with all thine heart; and lean not unto thine own understanding. In all thy ways acknowledge Him, and He shall direct thy paths."

At 7:00 a.m. contact was made with the pilot in Nyankunde. He said the weather locally had improved, and he planned to be at Punia for midday. Again Maud packed her case expecting to be gone for only two weeks. With the other passengers and work party they again made their way through the thick mud to the airfield.

The M.A.F. plane arrived at noon as promised. The pilot said the weather between Kisangani and Punia was atrocious, and he had used up most of his fuel as he had to detour round many storms. He thought of abandoning the landing in Punia as it was raining heavily everywhere else. Providentially there was a break in the clouds at Punia, and he slipped the plane below the cloud cover and was able to make a safe landing. However, with the deteriorating weather conditions they had to be on their way immediately.

The baggage and equipment which was brought on the light aircraft was hastily unloaded, and the passengers embarked and secured their safety belts. Maud waved her farewells to her friends from the small window and after some revving of the engine, the plane roared down the runway and up into the grey angry clouds.

Soon the cooler air at seven thousand feet gave some respite from the sticky heat below as they flew above the low ceiling of dark rain clouds below. After more than two hours in the air the plane landed in the midst of a tropical downpour at Nebobongo to refuel. The weather had not improved but in spite of the rain, Maud and other passengers disembarked from the plane to meet some local believers. Maud enjoyed this short visit at Nebobongo, for the introduction to her missionary career started here in this very area.

In less than an hour the plane took off again for the short hop to Isiro where several of the missionaries awaited their arrival. It was good to see colleagues who had come from all parts of the Congo and several who had just arrived back from their enforced furlough in their respective countries. This was an opportunity to catch up on everybody's news and to compare notes of what was happening in other parts of the country. Some missionary families were glad for their children to spend time with other missionary children. So much was happening all over Congo that everyone had plenty to talk about. All were concerned about the heightening tension throughout the country and especially in the eastern region.

The designated time for the conference in Isiro was passing quickly, and there was much for every one to do besides visiting and talking. The missionaries had gathered primarily for the annual Field meetings. Reports were given by missionaries and church leaders. Together they prayed and planned for the development of the work in the various regions. Much of the precious free time was spent buying supplies for every one returning to their respective mission stations.

On August 2, 1998 the president of the churches associated with WEC had to travel approximately two thousand miles to the Congolese Capital, Kinshasa, to meet with other national church leaders in order to re-register the mission and missionaries. To do this it was necessary for all the missionaries to give him their passports for them to obtain official validation in Kinshasa so that they could remain in the country. The missionaries were quite an international mix of Germans, Americans, French, Dutch, Canadians and British. No one likes to part with his passport, but it was government procedure and they had to conform.

The day after the church president left for Kinshasa a broadcast on BBC World Service reported trouble on the Rwanda border and west of Kinshasa. This report intensified the missionaries' focus on prayer for the situation. On the following morning another report confirmed what had been heard on the BBC. A MAF pilot transporting missionaries was informed that all airports were closed and the borders were sealed. The pilot was forced to return to Nyankunde where the missionaries disembarked from the foiled flight.

Word came through from reliable sources outside Congo that all missionaries had to be evacuated immediately. Many missionaries farther east than Isiro had already been taken to Uganda to escape the spreading rebellion. This urgent instruction to evacuate Isiro left the WEC missionaries in a dilemma. Their passports were in the possession of the church leader in Kinshasa and without a passport it was impossible to gain exit visas from Congo nor access into Uganda, Kenya or any other neighbouring country. Permission to leave was sought and denied them by local authorities, and furthermore, the church leaders were opposed to the sudden evacuation of the missionaries.

As the hours passed the pressure grew. Missionaries were concerned for each other, and all were especially anxious for those families with young children. Earnest prayer was made that God's hand would protect them all - Africans and missionaries alike. Notwithstanding the pressure and stress of the situation the same prevailing peace that Maud had experienced after the threats and danger at Mulita still prevailed in her heart.

The mission staff at Isiro maintained daily communication with their respective embassies in Nairobi where they were seeking to influence the Congolese authorities to give permission for the foreigners to leave. There was a growing unsettled feeling among the missionary community in Isiro. After more than a week of living with persistent uncertainty whether they would be leaving Congo or returning to their respective mission stations, the missionaries finally received a startling communication on Thursday August 13th. It reported that thousands of rebel soldiers were near and the missionaries should leave Isiro immediately. The communication also advised that they take cover and hide in the forest while trying to make their way to Nebobongo where it would be easier to evacuate them by air.

The shock of the announcement stunned everyone. Fear and panic were written on several faces and perhaps these seemed justified following such intimidating news. Mothers wept for their children while husbands comforted their wives. Missionaries assured each other that the Lord was in control of the situation and He would bring them through. However, all were mindful of the horrific atrocities in former years when many colleagues lost their lives in similar rebellions. There were spontaneous seasons of simple but earnest prayer. Many of these prayers were mingled with tears.

The missionaries collected what few belongings they could carry and during Thursday and Friday made their way to Nebobongo by various modes of transport. In Nebobongo the missionary families tried to stay together. They learned there was also a group of Wycliffe missionaries waiting evacuation from Nebobongo. Further word from Kenya informed them that two planes would be sent to evacuate all the missionaries and for them to be ready for immediate departure.

There was an added blow for Maud that Saturday evening. During the course of the late afternoon news came through on the BBC World Service of a massive car bomb in Omagh, near to Maud's home town in Northern Ireland. Some of her family shopped in Omagh on Saturday. Just after dark she learned that twenty-eight people lost their lives in the explosion and hundreds were injured. This added more stress to what Maud already felt in the crisis at Nebobongo.

It was with a broken heart that Maud earnestly sought the Lord for comfort and reassurance. She wept and prayed for her family and friends back home. She also prayed for God to protect both missionary and national alike in the ugly developments that were unfolding in Nebobongo. Her Bible readings brought the comfort and reassurance that she had prayed for. The New Testament reading was the account of Paul surviving the shipwreck in Acts 27:22. Paul declared, "I exhort you to be of good cheer for there shall be no loss of any man's life among you..." This word gave confidence to Maud that Jesus was the "Lord of the storm."

Opening the Old Testament to the book of Psalms Maud read Psalm 107 and found that this complemented what she had been reading in Acts 27. The Lord is the One who "makes the storm a calm" and when His people cry "He brings them to their desired haven." (Psalm 107:29,30)

With such reassurance sleep came a little easier that night and gave some respite to her exhausted body.

Early on Sunday morning the adrenaline was flowing again when the missionaries awoke to the same tense atmosphere that seem to hang over Nebobongo with the threat of impending invasion from the advancing rebels. After prayer and some light breakfast on Sunday morning the missionaries assembled again at the airport. One of the lady missionaries waited behind at the mission house in Nebobongo where she maintained radio communication with the MAF in Kenya.

That morning both the Wycliffe and WEC missionaries assembled at the airstrip in expectation of flights that morning. The anxious hours slipped by so slowly with no planes in sight. The uneasy group of missionaries waited every minute for news of the incoming flights. Even as they assembled and prayed in Nebobongo the church leaders were still opposed to the missionaries' withdrawal from Congo and voiced their opposition quite strongly. Their pleas for the missionaries to stay added to the dilemma they faced. On one hand the missionaries looked at the Africans who beckoned on them to stay. On the other hand their hearts were torn for the missionary children who were crying without being able to appreciate why there was so much tension and concern.

As the hours slipped by the morning tropical sun steadily followed its course to its noonday zenith in the cloudless sky. The air was hot and humid. Little groups gathered in what shade was available but even then it was hot and sticky. The small airstrip hewn out of the forest had no sanitary conditions and the long wait in sweltering heat made life very uncomfortable for all. The children at times were restless but behaved exceptionally well in spite of the distressing conditions.

Unknown to them two planes, piloted by missionaries, were already in the air. One aircraft belonged to Samaritan's Purse and the other to the United Nations Air Aid. Not long into their flight the pilots were forced to turn back as permission to land in Congo was denied. By radio transmission the pilots insisted that they should proceed with their flight to Nebobongo for the waiting missionaries. The Congolese authorities boldly replied that if they ventured into the air space near Nebobongo the two planes would be shot down and the missionaries would be taken hostage. The pilots felt they had no option but to return to Nairobi.

Just when they turned tail to abort the flight their radio transmission was intercepted and another voice interjected giving authoritative instructions for the pilots to proceed to Nebobongo as planned for the situation was too grave to turn back. The missionaries must be rescued from Nebobongo. The unidentified voice was both commanding and impressive. The pilots were told that if they failed to continue with their mission the missionaries' lives would be in danger.

It was a brave and bold decision for the two pilots to venture their light and non-combative planes into hostile airspace. However, they felt they owed it to their stranded colleagues. High above Africa's jungle they turned their aircraft again and headed into Congolese airspace to continue their rescue mission. It was later learned that the radio interception came from missionaries who were in contact with foreign embassies outside Congo and were monitoring the flights and communications.

The lady missionary listening by radio at the mission house in Nebobongo finally received word that the planes were coming in and would land at midday. She was told that all the missionaries should be ready for immediate departure.

When this news arrived at the airstrip there was increased excitement and agitation. The airstrip personnel had also heard the transmission informing them that the planes were due to land at noon. The news spread quickly and soon was greatly embellished by lies and rumour. Many young Africans who crowded at the airstrip began to hurl insults at the missionaries calling them traitors and cowards. It was even more hurtful when some Christians joined in the taunts and accused the missionaries of being spies. A leader of the church in Nebobongo came and told the missionaries to tell the pilots not to land. They were not welcome.

The airstrip manager spoke to the missionaries and told them that he would not allow the planes to touch down. He threatened to scatter empty oil drums on the airstrip to impede the aircraft landing. The missionaries pleaded with the airstrip manager to allow the planes to land but he stubbornly refused to relent. The tension grew and the situation became very volatile with the angry crowd threatening riot.

To try and defuse the situation some of the male missionaries tried to reason with the airstrip manager. They shared with him how grave the situation was with the rebels approaching ever nearer. They also pointed out to him that the missionaries, far from deserting the country, planned to return to Congo as soon as possible to continue to help the people with their medical and social programme. The manager still refused to agree to their request.

When Nehemiah, the man who rebuilt the broken walls of Jerusalem, pleaded in the presence of the King, he established a habit which all of us have learned to emulate in crisis times; "So I prayed to the God of heaven."(Nehemiah 2:4)   The missionaries followed Nehemiah's pattern and continually sent momentary prayers to heaven asking for God's intervention.

Shortly before noon the airstrip manager finally eased his aggressive attitude when he recognized that the missionary pilots meant to come down. Exactly at midday the drone of the two planes could be heard overhead in the sky. The imminent arrival of the aircraft heightened the crowd's harassment of the assembled missionaries. Frustrated by the taunts of the menacing crowd some missionaries wept while they tried to encourage each other. The children were clearly upset. Mothers hugged their crying children while husbands drew a comforting arm around their wives' shoulders.

By radio the missionary pilots instructed the missionaries to display two white sheets on the ground near the airstrip to indicate it was safe to land. Several of the missionaries put these in place as requested. When the irritate mob saw what was happening one man defiantly ran out and snatched the sheets. This left the pilots with a measure of uncertainty. Was it safe to land or not?

The answer to that question was given very speedily. Maud was carrying a white anorak coat for use in the colder climate after the evacuation. A Wycliffe missionary shouted, " Maud, give me your white coat."

Hurriedly Maud threw the coat into the missionary's grasp and he placed it where the sheets had been and stood guard over it. The pilots above saw the white coat on the ground and received the positive message it was meant to relay.

After circling above the airstrip the aircraft lowered their landing gear and came swooping in low over Nebobongo just clearing above the houses near the mud runway.

The Samaritan's Purse plane was the first to land. In a cloud of dust it taxied to where the group of foreigners were huddled together. The Wycliffe missionaries boarded the first plane. The United Nations Air Aid plane was next to land and the WEC missionaries lost no time in scrambling aboard the aircraft. Their hasty embarkation was accompanied by the taunting throng who continued to threaten to bomb the aircraft and kill the missionaries.

The whole operation on the ground only took seven minutes but for those involved it seemed like three hours. The aircraft gathered speed down the airstrip throwing up clouds of dust in their track until the planes lifted into the air. It was only when the aircraft climbed above the clouds that there was a sense of relief. This was spontaneously expressed around the aircraft with audible calls of "Amen" and "Praise the Lord." Others just wept.

The two planes and their precious cargo were not finally out of danger until one and a half hours later when they passed out of Congolese airspace and headed towards Nairobi. A warm and cordial welcome awaited them there by other missionaries who had escaped from Congo earlier.

The news that followed in succeeding weeks justified the missionaries' hasty evacuation. Horrific news reports spoke of mass looting and killings in Nebobongo and other towns in eastern Congo. Many believers had to hide in the dense forest. Pastors and believers were killed. Mission property was plundered and containers of equipment stolen. The news that filtered out from Mulita was also disconcerting. Congo was in the throes of a reckless civil war.

The term in the Congo was much shorter than Maud Kells or the other missionaries had anticipated. Nevertheless, when Maud looked back on the alarming and unforgettable episode during the summer of 1998 she remembered several lessons she had learned about her experience in war weary Congo.

LESSONS FOR TIMES OF FEAR AND DANGER.

Fear plays a big part in all our lives. It is one of the paramount emotions we experience in childhood and it remains with us through our adolescence and into adulthood. Fear was the first outward evidence and manifestation of the effect of disobedience in the Garden of Eden. Adam's first recorded words after his disobedience were his admission to God, "I heard thy voice in the garden and was afraid." Fear was the first symptom of sin. From that day fear has played its part in all our lives.

Frequently we applaud people's bravery and ridicule their fears. However, history shows that the bravest men have also been fearful men. Moses was brave enough to defend a Hebrew slave yet he fled Egypt in fear of his life. David facing Goliath was the epitome of courage and heroism. However, David's Psalms are filled with his expressions of fear and foreboding. Similarly Elijah, Daniel and the Hebrew children manifested extraordinary courage in the face of danger but they also experienced fear.

Undoubtedly, many fears are very unhealthy. In our modern and complex world there are people who suffer from all sorts of phobias and these fears rob them of normal living. While it is true that fear can be cowardly and spring from ignorance or a lack of faith, yet this is not so with all fear. Some fears are healthy and are justified. It is proper that we should fear fire and have a healthy respect for the ocean. When faced with any danger whether it be with fire, water or threat, our fears justifiably cause us to act in the interests of personal safety. This is right and proper.

The most important aspect of fear is that we should fear God. It was said of Oliver Cromwell that he was the bravest man that ever lived. When asked what was the secret of his bravery Cromwell replied, "I have learned from the Word of God that if you fear God you need fear nothing else."

Charles Spurgeon is reputed to have said, "There are two ways of handling fear. In the words of David we can say 'I will trust and not be afraid.' Alternatively, also in other words of David we can say, 'At what time I am afraid I will trust in the Lord.'"

Maud Kells and her missionary friends dedicated their lives to the Lord for His work in Africa. They were aware of the dangers they might face. Former colleagues of these missionaries who remained in Congo during a previous rebellion paid the ultimate sacrifice of martyrdom. For Maud it was a matter of saying, "I will trust in the Lord and not be afraid." However, when danger was thrust upon them and threats made against them it was a matter of saying, "At what time I am afraid I will trust in the Lord."

In the light of the nightmare experience in which Maud and her friends proved that God is always faithful, Maud remembered the following:

1. Inevitably we all make plans. We plan in our work, for our homes and make preparations for our future. Plans are a necessary part in all our lives. However, Maud, who had planned to stay in Congo longer than four months, was able to trace that above her planning there was a higher and sovereign hand shaping her life and arranging events for her and her colleagues. She learned that it "is God who works in us both to will and to do of His good pleasure." (Philippians 2:13)

2. The work God has given to us is not our work. We are like the sheep dogs who obey the Master Shepherd and serve the sheep. The flock is His. The field is His. We are His. He cares for us and He cares for all His flock.

3. We should not be surprised when we face hard times. (See Philippians 1:27) When faced with danger Maud and the other missionaries were

confronted with a great predicament. Although they had gone to the Congo to serve the Lord and work with the national church, at what stage should the missionary act in the interests of personal safety while remaining true to his calling? There is a fine balance between our responsibility to duty and our responsibility to personal safety. While we trust in the Lord for protection we must not be fool-hardy to expose ourselves and others to unnecessary risk and danger. When faced with impending danger we must not disregard the warnings nor the advice and experience of others. Maud and the other missionaries are grateful for those missionary pilots who heroically jeopardized their own lives to rescue their colleagues. Hundreds of people were praying for the missionaries' welfare. However, they all learned that ultimately safety comes from the Lord.

4. The repeated evacuations from the Congo have taught Maud and many other missionaries the futility and hollowness of earthly possessions. Material wealth matters little and has little value when confronted with life and death situations. If all your possessions were wrapped up in five kilos of baggage how rich would you be? The nearer we approach eternity the less material things matter.

5. Maud Kells and her colleagues learned that when we are in danger we are not alone. God is not only present but He is in control and He will work out His plan.

Trust Him with your life.

Chapter two

Please Release Me, Let Me Go

IT WAS TUESDAY NIGHT AT A TERRACE HOUSE IN A NARROW STREET ON BELFAST'S EAST SIDE. MORE THAN TWENTY PEOPLE, men and women of varying ages, crowded into the rearranged living room. Some were sitting on chairs, a long sofa, easy chairs and stools. The more agile squatted on the carpeted floor. Several were quite well groomed while others were casually dressed and a few, still in their working duds, had just arrived from their place of employment.

The camaraderie of these folk was clearly evidenced by their banter and teasing of each other which is wholly typical of their Belfast humour. Many had been life-long friends and had known each other in surroundings and circumstances very much contrasted from this present house gathering. They were all converted and reformed alcoholics. Most of them I got to know during my nine years of Christian ministry in Belfast. Let me introduce you to several of them.

❖ ❖ ❖

Pamela, in whose house these friends met, is a housewife and a mother of two children. She was born, raised and educated on a local housing estate, a few miles away from her present dwelling. Pamela was the youngest girl in a large family. Her mother and father went through an acrimonious divorce when she was only an infant.

By that time most of Pamela's older brothers and sisters had left home to be married or to seek employment elsewhere. Forsaken by her intoxicated father Pamela was vulnerable to the legacy which many drunkards pass on to their family. Alcohol may not only leave a person with an unsteady and unbalanced step, it will also create an unbalanced home where unbalanced social order often deprives children and dependants of many of the necessities of life.

Unknown to her mother, Pamela became very irregular in her attendance at the Primary School and then later the High School. Frequently she and her friends absconded from their classes to secretly drink cider, shandy and beer in secluded alley ways. Just after her twelfth birthday Pamela, for the first time in her young life, got drunk and fell into an intoxicated stupor. When she recovered she felt she had been initiated into normal adulthood. Most of the adults she knew drank excessively.

During her early teenage years Pamela and her friends hung around bars and clubs and swilled inordinate amounts of booze until they had to be carried home drunk most weekends. When Pamela was fifteen she met a boy in a pub and was infatuated by the attention he paid to her. Roy, who was two years older than Pamela, had been to Manchester United for trials as a football apprentice. Homesickness prematurely ruled out a future in soccer and soon he was back in Belfast with Pamela, his teenage sweetheart. The young couple became firm drinking pals and two years later they were married.

After a brief spell living with Pamela's parents they set up home. Visits to pubs, clubs and drinking at home continued unabated. The young newly-weds did not think their action was outrageous nor abnormal for most of their friends indulged in the same irrepressible obsession with alcoholic beverages. Many drinking companions came to stay at their home and together they wallowed in a booze-up night after night and Pamela and Roy were seldom sober.

The weekends were spent on one continuous binge from morning to night and frequently, when the light of dawn broke on Sunday mornings, several drunken buddies lay sleeping on the floor or on a couch in the living room.

Money was not plentiful but often they waived food to buy more liquor. Although they drank constantly they still had to face their place of employment the following day. Pamela felt like a hamster trapped in a cage and climbing the treadmill in an endless and aimless cycle that got her nowhere. It seemed as if she was chasing after the wind and catching nothing. Week after week her hard earned money was soon squandered in order to buy more vodka and spirits to placate her appetite for more drink.

Inevitably her life paid a heavy price. Booze got such a grip on Pamela that during daylight hours her body trembled and almost convulsed until she was able satisfy her slavish craving with yet another slug on a bottle of vodka. In the shop where she worked she often had to recline on a couch until her head stopped spinning or her stomach ceased heaving. She loved the bottle and the booze at night but loathed it by day.

Pamela was not a selfish person and she readily shared with her friends the little she had. However, her binges on booze made her what she did not want to be. Roy and Pamela had two children but her addiction to liquor frequently left her home bereft of the many basic comforts that other families enjoyed. She felt she was depriving her children of the happiness that had previously eluded Pamela as a child. She was convinced that drink was making her into a horrible monster which robbed and denied her children of what they needed and deserved.

Her drinking habit also created a low sense of self-esteem and she began to hate herself. There were feelings of guilt and shame for what she was doing to herself, to her husband, to her children and to her home. This guilt made her feel like a prisoner trapped in a dark dungeon of despair with no possible escape. The only relief Pamela could find from these irrepressible feelings of guilt and shame was to block out such nightmarish thoughts by returning to binge again and again on still more bottles of vodka.

By the time Pamela was in her mid-twenties she was trapped in a vicious cycle with no apparent escape. Her life was deficient of love, respectability and self-esteem. She made many half-hearted attempts to reform but felt chained to the liquor bottle and despaired for her life and family. Half of her wanted to give up the bottle but the other half wanted to hang on to the drink. She knew no other way to live. Pamela was at rock bottom. Life for her was painful and aimless. She could find no way out of this mess.

❖ ❖ ❖

Elaine is a twin in a family of four children in which she is the only daughter. Out-numbered by boys at home Elaine was very much a tomboy who engaged in boyish activities and was more at home in their company than with other girls. Her Mum and Dad were typical hardworking Belfast people who reared their children in the midst of Ulster's turbulent troubles during the 1970s. However, they were functional alcoholics who in spite of holding down good jobs, spent most of their leisure time drinking beer and spirits. Every weekend they were totally intoxicated and stupefied because of their addiction to alcohol.

While she yet a teenager Elaine met up with the wrong company at school and soon she was introduced to beer parties and drunken revellries. At first it seemed to be good fun. The kids pooled their money and one of them volunteered to go into a wine store where he bought as much beer as the gang could afford. The juveniles then headed off to the embankment at the River Lagan or to a back alley way where they downed tin after tin of beer. When Elaine's friends could drink no more she habitually drained their tins and drank the last drop.

For her the chief aim of a night out at parties and discos was to get blocked out of her mind. Elaine was disappointed if she did not end up so drunk she had to be carried home. On some occasions she was too drunk to face home and just lay down and fell asleep where she was.

At home her parents could say little to discourage their daughter taking these degenerate steps down the liquor highway for they also enjoyed their boozing and accepted drinking as an inevitable development in their family.

As an impressionable teenager Elaine was also sucked into the local paramilitary culture and soon was engrossed in illegal activities. One of the supposed privileges of being accepted into such a fraternity was the availability of plenty of booze. Elaine indulged to the limit. Before long these paramilitary associations brought her into contact with drugs and the twin addictions of drugs and drink seduced Elaine into a promiscuous lifestyle.

Quite often the police were called to break up a drunken brawl in which Elaine inevitably was involved. On one occasion she was arrested and thrown into the back of a military Land Rover. Drunk and irresponsible, she assaulted the two officers who had apprehended her by kicking them as they entered the vehicle. She was charged with disorderly conduct and subsequently heavily fined for her aggressive behaviour. Stealing cars and joy-riding while under the influence of drink was another crime Elaine and her friends engaged in. It was a mercy such irresponsible behaviour did not result in herself or a third party being killed in a horrific accident.

As she was further absorbed into the camaraderie and activity of the paramilitary organisation her life was under constant threat from other terrorist groupings. With her partner she lived in a house which was secured by reinforced doors and burglar alarms. Replica automatic weapons were conveniently placed at their bedside. Even then, her home was badly damaged by an explosive device planted at her front door. They moved to another house in East Belfast.

The pressure of such a hectic lifestyle forced Elaine to more dependency on hard liquor and drugs which robbed her of any vestige of self-esteem and social development. She so hated herself that she refused to look in the mirror. In total despair Elaine wanted to trigger the self-destruct button of her life and she became suicidal. It seemed there were no other options for this distraught girl. There was no escape from this profligate cesspool of drink, dope and terrorism that was dragging Elaine farther and farther down until it seemed that she had gone beyond the point of no return.

❖ ❖ ❖

Wee Billy and Ruby are Elaine's parents. They both held very good jobs and for many years enjoyed the outdoor activities of fishing and camping. However, both had been introduced to a web of alcohol abuse which had been so glamorized that it seemed to be the accepted and sophisticated thing to do.

Billy enjoyed his evenings out at several bars in East Belfast. Some nights he was so drunk that he staggered home on his bare feet and didn't realise he had left his shoes in the pub. A local police officer told me that on Saturday nights no one in Billy's street dared to leave their milk bottles at their doorstep for Billy smashed every milk bottle he found as he stumbled home up Ravenhill Avenue after midnight.

Alcohol made a fool of Ruby who, when sober, was a cheerful, very kind and considerate person. However, when under the influence of alcohol Ruby became schizophrenic and underwent a change of personality whereby she became quite aggressive. As a result of this aggression in company the family decided to bring Ruby's alcoholic beverages to her house so that she could routinely intoxicate herself at home every night from Thursday through to Sunday. Frequently so much alcohol was brought to their house that Billy, Ruby, their four children and some visiting cousins were all totally intoxicated.

Holidays were just one continual binge which ended in a drunken stupor every night. Recurrently at home Ruby had to be carried to bed or she slept the night away on the sofa where she had gone unconscious. On one unforgettable Christmas Eve Billy and Ruby were so stoned with booze that the children had to find their own Christmas presents which Ruby when sober had hidden from their prying eyes. Christmas Day started with another cycle of excessive drinking that lasted through to the New Year.

Although alcohol had become the most important thing in their lives Billy would not admit that he was an alcoholic. He loved his drink and the company at the bar and felt he had it all under control. He was able to continue in his work where he earned good money which provided the means to acquire more booze to fuel and satisfy his passion for alcohol. Furthermore, all the people that Billy knew were boozers and he felt that this was normal behaviour for a man of his standing.

Not so with Ruby. She felt so wrapped up in her overwhelming habit that it became the consuming passion of her life. She was a slave to the bottle. Although she would love to have been free from this fixation with alcohol there seemed no way to stop. She felt she was on an addict's merry-go-round and could not get off.

❖ ❖ ❖

Norman and Linda lived in the heart of the Woodstock Road with their only son. Although young Gary arrived home to tell his mother and father that he had become a Christian, his parents had no regard for religion in their lives. They were just glad he was not following in their footsteps. Norman and Linda were more at home in the pubs and social clubs of East Belfast and sadly, like many of their friends, Thursday through to Sunday was one continual binge which resulted in complete intoxication.

While the on-looker may find it difficult to see any sense or satisfaction in such a lifestyle, yet for Norman and Linda this was their idea of living. Norman was never more at home than when he not only drank in a bar, but had the opportunity to work in one.

Linda's mother became ill and young Gary led his grandmother to faith in Jesus Christ. Her death shortly afterwards had a devastating effect on Linda who knew no other way to drown her sorrows other than by the consumption of more alcoholic drink. Stress and tension from the bereavement resulted in the drunken binges ending in rows between Norman and Linda and often at the end of several days drinking and fighting their home was left like a battlefield.

During all this time Gary was praying for his mother and father. One night he stepped into the midst of a terrible brawl between his parents and when he saw the state of his mother he told her she needed to find God and get out of the mess of drink and violence. Linda longed to abandon the drink but did not know how.

❖ ❖ ❖

Jake and Audrey lived in the same street as Norman and Linda. They had heard about Linda's conversion but felt it could never happen to them. Audrey had no interest in alcohol during her adolescence. It never even played a part in her life after she met and married Jake when she was twenty-years old.

She was happy at home looking after her three children and only indulged in alcoholic drinks when Jake brought home a carry-out on Saturday nights. However, there was a dramatic turn in this pattern after their youngest son started school. Both Jake and Audrey started to go out for a few drinks on Thursdays at lunch time when they got their wages. Soon they both got so hooked on the bottle that they continued drinking all day.

Before long both of them were drinking seven days a week. Everything went to the wall. Audrey's parents and sister had been converted just about the time Audrey and Jake took to the bottle and it broke the parents' hearts to see their daughter slipping into alcoholic addiction. However, Jake and Audrey were unconcerned about it. They loved their drink and just had to have it.

Money was not plentiful for Jake and Audrey but alcohol emptied their pockets and destroyed their home. Soon the children seldom saw their mother sober. Jake's body began to show the tell-tale marks of addiction. The couple had been caught in a hopeless spiral of addiction that was dragging them down and there seemed no way of stopping the worsening deterioration.

❖ ❖ ❖

These are only a few of our friends who gather at this cottage meeting in a terraced house in East Belfast. Watching their lives over a number of years I made the following observations.

I. ALCOHOLISM IS AN ADDICTION

Pamela confessed that alcohol was an artificial masking of her real problems. Alcoholism and drug addiction is an attempt to meet one's emotional needs through the use of alcohol or drugs. Many adults, teenagers and increasing numbers of children are turning to these twin vices in a bid to cope with stress, depression, loneliness, rejection and abandonment. They are deluded into assuming that these addictive substances will blunt the pain of anxiety and tension or give hope and independence. Addiction to these abuses is often symptomatic of deeper social and emotional problems.

Elaine, like most substance addicts, admitted she indulged in the consumption of alcohol and drugs because she enjoyed it. Initially the addict may get a kick out of their habit but the pattern is predictable. The more they consume the greater becomes their desire for more drugs or drink until the body begins to crave satisfaction from the habitual activity. The experience makes them high and gives them short-term relief from despair and reality.

As Jake and Audrey discovered, addiction often results in creating many physical, social and emotional problems. It can also create domestic unrest and bring misery to the home. Self-esteem, sound judgement, physical well-being, employment and financial security are only some of the casualties of these addictions. The addict's inadequacies, faults and problems are greatly intensified and sometimes the person may become suicidal.

The best step to escape from alcoholism is total abstinence right from the start. Every alcoholic starts with the first drink. Total abstinence nips the problem at the root.

2. THE BIBLE HAS THE ANSWER FOR THE ADDICT AND HIS
    ADDICTION.

All those who gathered in the terraced house in East Belfast discovered that there is hope for alcoholics and modern drug abusers. How silly it is for those people who allege that the Bible is out of date and not related to present times. Such allegations can only flow from people who do not read the Word of God. I have found that the Scriptures are more up to date in addressing these problems than we can ever imagine. The Bible addresses the problems of the heart and one thing we discover in our study of the Bible is that people basically have not changed very much in their hearts and habits. Biblical history throws up to us a change in culture, customs and language but the age-old problem of the corrupt heart is still with us today.

The Gentile world of the New Testament was characterized by reckless debauchery and indulgence in many vices. Paul was not silent in addressing these matters. He said, " Be not drunk with wine, wherein is excess. But be filled with the Spirit." (Ephesians 5:18) He further cautioned, "Let us walk honestly, as in the day; not in rioting and drunkenness." (Romans 13:13)

Solomon's Proverbs are permeated with references and commands to those who abuse themselves with intoxicating substances.

Wine is a mocker, strong drink is raging: and whosoever is deceived thereby is not wise. (Proverbs 20:1)

Who hath woe? who hath sorrow? who hath contentions? who hath babbling? who hath wounds without cause? who hath redness of eyes? They that tarry long at the wine; they that go to seek mixed wine.   Look not thou upon the wine when it is red, when it giveth his colour in the cup, when it moveth itself aright. At the last it biteth like a serpent, and stingeth like an adder. (Proverbs 23:29-32)

Addiction is not something that is limited to a bottle of alcoholic drink.   Many today are trapped by chemical abuse, either by pills, injections or nasal snorting of powders. Football legends George Best, Paul Merson and Tony Adams are only a few of the high profile stars who have succumbed to substance addictions.   Paul Merson recently admitted on television that he is an alcoholic, a drug tripper and a gambling addict who needed the sort of help that money could not buy.

These addictions are not the peculiar plight of a back alley society or sleazy dens of iniquity. Addictions can also work their way into beautiful homes where normal children engage in children's activities. It creeps into the prosperous offices of major companies. Prisons, army garrisons, schools and even some athletic clubs have had their share of those who became enslaved to some form of addiction.

Amazingly we have emerged into the twenty-first century surrounded by our sophisticated technology that has provided most homes with the latest computerized facilities and furnished with boundless information.

For all this modern development we have not yet been able to tame one of the most ancient vices that has enslaved men and women for thousands of years. At the bottom of every bottle of liquor lies the potential of a broken home, a ruined marriage and the destruction of a life. Surely poison is in the bottle.

The apostle Paul provides the prime reason why chemical and substance abuse are wrong.

What? know ye not that your body is the temple of the Holy Ghost which is in you, which ye have of God, and ye are not your own? For ye are bought with a price: therefore glorify God in your body, and in your spirit, which are God's." (I Corinthians 6:19,20)

Why is God so against drunkenness and drug abuse? Because such vices are rebels of human life. They are a threat to the marriage bond, arch-enemies of the family unit and are against individual welfare.

Nevertheless, the same God who repudiates addiction also provides the message to liberate the addict and enable him to overcome his addiction. The Bible teaches that there is deliverance from the sordid and destructive habits of humanity in Jesus Christ and not in chemicals. Jesus Christ said,

"Then said Jesus to those Jews which believed on him, If ye continue in my word, then are ye my disciples indeed;   And ye shall know the truth, and the truth shall make you free. They answered him, We be Abraham's seed, and were never in bondage to any man: how sayest thou, Ye shall be made free? Jesus answered them, Verily, verily, I say unto you, Whosoever committeth sin is the servant of sin. And the servant abideth not in the house for ever: but the Son abideth ever. If the Son therefore shall make you free, ye shall be free indeed." (John 8:29-32)

Charles Swindoll rightly points out "No addiction – I repeat, no addiction is more powerful than the power of the Almighty. Never forget that His power stills the stormy seas and heals diseases and casts out demons.   In fact it is the same power that once raised Jesus from the dead."

IT IS IMPORTANT TO BE AVAILABLE TO HELP THE ADDICT.

To help an addict you will need a lot of determined and persevering love. The first time I spoke to Jake about the Gospel he was well-oiled. My attempt to witness to him was futile. We all have had experience of trying to help a person abused by drink or drugs while they were still under the influence of their addiction. It is almost always a fruitless exercise and sometimes counter-productive. I have found it is better to arrange to meet with them when they are sober.

My experience of dealing with addicts is that they generally do not feel good about their drug or drink-induced state and the problems it creates. Nevertheless, I have also discovered that alcoholics are frequently dishonest and deceitful about their addiction. They will do everything to try and cover up. Until the abuser hits "rock bottom" he will blame other people and other circumstances but you will not get to the core of his problem. He must admit his problem and his inadequacy to help himself. The abuser must also be willing to make a commitment to quit the fixation for good.

I have always tried to be frank with the addict without being critical. There may be underlying roots such as guilt, failure, stress, or promiscuity that led the person to addiction.

Use the Bible as a tool to present the Gospel to the addict but not as a club to batter him. Emphasize that God promises not only to forgive our sins but also to purify and cleanse us from all unrighteousness. (IJohn 1:9) The power of the Gospel is the dynamic of God to change a man or woman and make them a new creature. The word "power" when associated with the Gospel in the New Testament is the word "dynamite." (Romans 1:16) Dynamite as we know it is the destructive release by an explosion. The dynamite of the Gospel is the re-creative power of God as demonstrated in the resurrection of the Saviour and the Gospel is able to put the life back together again.

Encourage the person to receive Jesus Christ as Saviour. (John 1:12)

Once the addict receives the Saviour he must not only sever all associations with drink and drunkards but encourage him to seek new relationships and friends at a Bible-believing church.   (2 Corinthians 5:17)

The Christian disciplines of daily prayer, Bible reading and meeting with other Christians are essentials for development in the new convert's Christian life. I try to provide the convert with suitable material to encourage Bible reading. Do not presume new converts know the Bible. When Pamela was converted she was bewildered when people began to speak freely about Noah's ark.   She had never heard of it.

Relapses are possible as Norman discovered. Warn the convert about the dangers of slipping back but emphasize that a relapse need not be final.   Be patient and optimistic. Assure the person that there is still forgiveness and a future for him. (I John 1:9; 2:1; Proverbs 28:13)

Always be available to help, encourage and to counsel. It may be demanding but it is rewarding.

Those who are hurting from substance abuse are aware of the burning sensation that takes hold of the addict for another drink. Sometimes it is awful beyond words. However, freedom from this strong chain that binds and enslaves the drunkard is also something too wonderful for words. God is stronger than any habit and He can and will give new life in Jesus Christ when the sinner repents from his sin and trusts Jesus Christ as his Saviour.

Having trusted Jesus Christ as Saviour learn to depend on Him every day. "For that which I do I allow not: for what I would, that do I not; but what I hate, that do I." (Romans 7:15) No one understands these words better than the alcoholic. Like our friends in Belfast they hated their habit and wanted to be better people with a better lifestyle.   Jesus Christ invites us, "Come unto me, all ye that labour and are heavy laden, and I will give you rest. Take my yoke upon you, and learn of me; for I am meek and lowly in heart: and ye shall find rest unto your souls." Transfer your dependence each day from yourself unto Him and remember Philippians 4:13 "I can do all things through Christ which strengtheneth me."

Speak to God in prayer each day. "Draw nigh to God, and he will draw nigh to you…" (James 4:8) "The LORD [is] nigh unto all them that call upon him, to all that call upon him in truth" Psalm 145:18. The Lord is constantly at your side and is never any further away than the prayer you utter. Ask God for strength for each day. When you fail ask God for forgiveness. Thank Him for his help. Learn to pray after the pattern the Lord taught in Matthew 6:9-13.

Read the Bible each day. The Bible is food for our souls. The Word of God will strengthen us and nourish us. When we pray we speak to God. When we read the Bible God speaks to us.

Take one day at a time. Often we become frightened and disheartened when we think of the future. Do not let the fears of tomorrow rob from your life today. Psalm 31 is a good guide for this - Our trust is in the Lord. (Psalm 31:1) Our troubles are known to the Lord. (Psalm 31:7) Our times are in His hands. (Psalm 31:15)

Engage in helping others. You will be amazed how much help you derive from helping others. Give your life over to the Lord to help those who are yet enslaved in the vice that held you.

❖ ❖ ❖

The case histories I described at the beginning of this chapter have an interesting story to tell. There was a dramatic change in all these lives. One evening Pamela had a visit from a distant relation, Jackie Scott, who told her of his conversion to Jesus Christ. He invited Pamela to the Sunday evangelistic service at Templemore Hall. At first Pamela treated Jackie's conversion with contempt as he also had an unsavoury past. He persisted in challenging Pamela to attend the evangelistic meeting and to his surprise Pamela, motivated more by defiance than desire, said she would go with him.

Entering church the following Sunday evening was like walking into another world. Most people who sat around Pamela in church were well-dressed and spoke freely of spiritual matters and no one reeked of alcohol. For her it seemed she was amongst aliens.

She was soon captivated by the singing of the hymns and choruses. Her interest was further deepened by the evangelistic preaching that followed. Pamela confessed that church did not make her feel good. She felt worse than ever about her addiction to drink. She was emotionally stirred but felt she was too much of a prisoner of booze to be reformed. She returned to her familiar circumstances at home and soon was in the company of her boozing friends. What a contrast from one company of people to another. Pamela longed to be free from the life she had known and the habits that bound her.

Impressed by what she experienced the previous week at Templemore Hall Pamela returned the following Sunday night. Again she felt deep shame for what drink and the evils associated with that lifestyle had done to her young life. At the end of the service I gave an invitation for those who would accept the Lord Jesus Christ. My wife Audrey led Pamela to Jesus Christ that evening.

To be converted is to be changed and what a change came over Pamela. The days that followed brought mixed feelings of doubt, fear and the hope that God would give her the strength to resist the dreaded bottle. There was conflict in her mind and body every day but her simple prayers and the prayers of her newly-acquired friends encouraged and enabled her to overcome the temptations.

Pamela worked with Elaine at a shop in their neighbourhood. They had been drinking pals and Elaine had often slept overnight on a floor in Pamela's house. Elaine was totally unchurched and at first was skeptical and cynical about Pamela's conversion. Hopeless and suicidal, Elaine observed that Pamela stayed clean from alcohol and spoke realistically and enthusiastically about spiritual matters.

Alone in her heavily protected bedroom, Elaine called out for God to help her. Several weeks later Elaine attended the evangelistic service at Templemore Hall. She felt even more alienated from church culture than Pamela and was very withdrawn and awkward when people tried to make her welcome. After the evangelistic preaching that Sunday evening Audrey, my wife, counselled Elaine and led her to faith in Jesus Christ.

The change in Elaine's life was radical. It needed to be for Elaine. The tentacles of her old life were tightly wrapped around her and no human will power could sever them. At first it was difficult to make the break from the drug and drink culture and the terrorist associations. Again Christians not only prayed for her but got alongside her to help and encourage in practical ways.

Elaine's conversion made many people sit up and take notice of the radical change in her life. The swearing and profane language stopped. The booze was replaced by a Bible. The paramilitary relationships were replaced by the fellowship at the church. Her parents could not believe that this was for real.

The impact challenged Billy, Elaine's Dad, and he quit drinking and began to take an interest in what was happening to Elaine down at the church. Ruby was not so sure. She continued to drink and get drunk in the seclusion of her home. Four months after Elaine's conversion she invited her Mum and Dad to special evangelistic meetings in Templemore Hall where both were led to personal faith in Jesus Christ in the same night.

The same night in which young Gary found his mother and father fighting, even though his mother was drunk, he took her to Billy and Patsy Alexander's home in Bangor. They counselled her and assured her that the Lord could set her free. When she sobered up the next day Linda was ashamed of her life and despairing of what drink was doing to her, to her home and to her husband. She fell on her knees and cried to God for help and mercy but did not know what to do. It was then she remembered that her friend Pamela Brown had been converted.

Pamela took her to Templemore Hall the following day and my wife led Linda to personal faith in Jesus Christ. Ten months later Norman also made a profession of faith.

The Lord spoke to Audrey, Jake's wife, while she was still in a bar. She left the lounge and headed for Linda's house. She told Linda that she was miserable with drink. Linda prayed with her and Audrey asked the Lord into her life. Nine months later Audrey led her husband Jake to the Lord in their own home.

The change in their lives was astounding. The family had been well-known in their area and news of these conversions made a big impact. Other alcoholics from the immediate area began to ask for help. Joan and Sharon took similar steps to receive the Lord Jesus Christ. They were not all success stories. Some returned to their old ways. Sadly, Norman has had many setbacks. He still stays sober for a long period and then hits the road for a binge that lasts for anything up to a week.

As a result of these cries for help John Brown of Stauros Foundation was invited to help and advise. This contact cemented a link between the Woodstock Road group and Stauros a Christian outreach organization which specializes in reaching alcoholics and substance abusers.

Pamela studied at Belfast Bible College and subsequently was accepted as a full-time worker with a Stauros Foundation. Elaine went to work in an outreach centre near to Dublin. It was there she met Woody Price, an American missionary. Since then Woody and Elaine got married and now they also are full-time workers with Stauros Foundation. Audrey and Ruby are also active workers with the same agency while Linda's and Norman's son Gary is an Elim pastor in Northern Ireland.

The simple testimony of these who have been abused by alcohol is that they have not stopped drinking. It is just that they have changed the fountain from which they drink. They have found in Jesus Christ a well of living water that springs up unto eternal life and they are now drinking from that fountain.

He breaks the power of cancelled sin.
He sets the prisoner free.
His blood can make the foulest clean.
His blood avails for me.

Chapter three

Bad News From The Doctor

IT WAS A COLD BRISK NOVEMBER NIGHT IN 1998. AUDREY AND I HAD FINISHED DINNER AND AS USUAL WE WERE RUSHING OUT to another meeting. Unexpectedly the door bell summoned our attention. Through the clear glass on the side panels of the door I could see it was Eric McCully, a missionary with Arab World Ministries. I knew he had just returned from the Yemen and assumed he was calling to fill me in with some news of his latest assignment.

Immediately the door opened Eric stepped back and let Gillian, his wife, enter first. As soon as she stepped into the hallway Gillian, a beautiful woman in her mid-thirties and a radiant Christian, dissolved in a flood of tears accompanied by heavy sobbing. Eric curled his arm around her shoulder to comfort his distressed wife and led her into our small family room. She leaned into my wife's open embrace and buried her head in Audrey's shoulder.

Through her tears and deep sobs Gillian tried to be coherent, "We have just come from Lagan Valley Hospital..." Her voice faltered.

"I have a lump...it is malignant."

Eric's head dropped with obvious grief to see his despairing wife so hurt with this appalling news. We were stunned and numbed. We tried to fight back the tears as Audrey sat down on the settee with Gillian.

This was the third case of bad news from the doctor in as many months at Banbridge Baptist Church. Louise, a fine Christian teacher, had been diagnosed with a malignant growth in September and was admitted to hospital for immediate surgery. In October Joan, a loving mother and devoted home maker, was crushed to learn that she had a malignant condition which needed surgical attention without delay. Now it was Gillian. Sadly, for her this was not the first time to receive bad news. This was almost a surreal duplication of events that had moulded Gillian's life in earlier years.

Sharon and Gillian are twins and share the distinction of being the oldest of four girls in their family. They were raised in a Christian home where Mum and Dad, Gordon and Doreen Crawford, took their girls to Finaghy Baptist Church. When Jimmy Slater spoke at the European Christian Mission camp for young people in 1976 Gillian came to know the Lord Jesus Christ as Saviour. There is no better environment than a Christian home for a new convert and even though she was in her middle teens, Gillian learned much of Christian values and priorities both from her parents and godly grandparents.

A year after Gillian's conversion the Crawford home was blessed by the arrival of baby Laura. She seemed to be the ideal "living doll" for her three sisters Sharon, Gillian and Joanne. They nursed her, cuddled her, fed her and played with their darling little sister. This help and attention was much appreciated by Mum who worked in the records office at Belvoir Park Hospital. It seemed the Crawford home was the epitome of all that was good and desirable in a close family unit.

It was just then that a dark cloud began to creep over Gordon's and Doreen's home. Not long after the birth of baby Laura, Doreen discovered a suspicious lump on her breast. She discounted any significance to the lump seeing she had recently given birth to a baby. Besides, her dad had just recently suffered a heart attack and to raise alarm in the family could be detrimental to his health. She opted to remain silent about her condition. However, after several months the lump was undiminished. Although she prayed about the matter it still caused her some secret anxiety. Even so, she still chose not to create any unnecessary upset in the family or to share her secret with Gordon.

Doreen's decision to conceal her physical condition was suddenly jolted on April 5th 1979. Gordon, without any warning, collapsed at home and almost immediately sank into a deep coma. There was great alarm in the family. Gordon was always looked up to as the healthy leader in the home. He was still unconscious and soaked with perspiration when the ambulance rushed him three miles to the Belfast City Hospital. After running some preliminary tests the doctors soon got to the bottom of Gordon's problem. He was diagnosed diabetic. After stabilizing his blood sugar balance he was introduced to a course of treatment and a completely new lifestyle.

The sudden onset of Gordon's illness not only shocked Doreen, it made her more conscious of her own vulnerability and the suspicious lump that she had hidden from the family. Two weeks after Gordon's collapse and while he was recovering in hospital Doreen felt she should disclose her secret to her husband. When she told him about the lump he was dumbfounded. He was even more aghast when Doreen told him that the offending lump had been there for nine months and had not diminished. He made her promise that she give it immediate attention and see the family doctor.

The doctor also was not pleased that Doreen had concealed this for so long and at once he made an early appointment at the same hospital where Gordon had spent several weeks as a patient.

After examination by a consultant Doreen was recommended for exploratory surgery. Before being given the anaesthetic Doreen had to sign a form permitting the surgeon to take radical action should the tumour prove to be malignant. Gordon Crawford and his little family prayed for his wife. Doreen was only thirty-nine years old and her four children needed their mummy.

Following the operation Doreen was taken to the recovery ward where she slowly regained consciousness. Gordon, still weak from his recent illness, apprehensively waited for news from the doctor. Was this a benign cyst or a malignant tumour? Soon the surgeon would emerge to disclose the news. Hearts were tense but prayers were fervent. As Doreen emerged out of her enforced sleep, her hand slowly and almost subconsciously moved towards the area of the surgery. Even in her dazed condition Doreen was anxious to know the result of the operation.

Gordon was invited to meet the surgeon in a nearby consulting room. The consultant was sympathetic but honest and confirmed Gordon's and Doreen's worst fears. "The lump was malignant and deep. We had to do a mastectomy on your wife and have taken away as much as we can. With treatment it is amazing what can be done. We will arrange for Doreen to see Mr. Abrahams at the Belvoir Park Hospital for a course of radiotherapy and chemotherapy."

The children visited mummy in hospital but were not fully aware of the gravity of the situation. Almost simultaneously Gordon started to attend the Diabetic Clinic at the Belfast's Royal Victoria Hospital while Doreen was taken to Belvoir Park Hospital every Monday for her course of prescribed treatment. Through these troubled times Gordon and Doreen never lost their confidence that the Lord was in control of their lives and the surrounding circumstances. They appreciated the pastoral assistance which Pastor George Crory and the friends at Finaghy Baptist Church gave them. As much as possible the ill-stricken family continued to play a part in the life of the fellowship at Finaghy.

One of the missionaries Gordon and Doreen Crawford supported was a young man who also belonged to the Finaghy Baptist Church. Eric McCully was converted at the same Church in 1979 and shortly after his conversion he went to serve the Lord on the Operation Mobilization ministry ship, Doulos. From their house in Orpen Park Doreen often took a gift round to Eric's house in Finaghy but due to her illness she was not able to make the journey. She asked Gillian to make the errand for her. Gillian did not know that the young man to whom she delivered the envelope would play a big part in her life. He would soon become her husband.

While Gordon's condition and treatment was stabilized, Doreen's health deteriorated. Over the next four years there were frequent visits to the hospital. One operation led to another and although hopes were sometimes raised, the general trend was declining health. Doreen's pituitary gland was removed in a vain attempt to stifle the advance of the destructive disease. It was easier for Doreen to make the adjustment to using a wheelchair than the dreaded thought of losing her hair. Earnestly she prayed that the Lord would not let her lose her hair. She never did. However, the cancer spread from her breast to her bones and then finally to her brain.

Added to Gordon's and Doreen's physical difficulties there were obvious problems with baby Laura. The girls cared for their baby sister but slowly it became obvious to those closest to her that she had not developed just as quickly as Gillian, Sharon or Joanne. At first it was thought she was a slow learner. Further consultation with the family doctor indicated that Laura's difficulties were more problematic than that. He recommended further investigation.

Doreen was too ill to attend clinics and hospital visits with her infant daughter Laura. Gordon was accompanied by Gillian or Sharon when they took the baby to visit Professor Norman Nevin, Northern Ireland's leading genetic specialist. After nearly two years of investigations the Crawfords' youngest daughter was eventually diagnosed as having Rett Syndrome, a neurological congenital disorder occurring only in females, which leaves them profoundly disabled for life. From her third year Laura needed special care in nursing homes designed and equipped for other patients with similar illnesses.

During the months and years of his wife's failing health and what might be naturally looked upon as adverse family circumstances, Doreen and Gordon did not question the Lord's ways. There were no such things as blaming God. The Crawford family unit was strong and their love for each other was strengthened more. They were not aware of stress although it must have been there. The Lord gave them grace for each day and strength for every contingency.

During the second week of August 1983 the World Athletic Championships were convened in Helsinki, Finland. Britain's Daly Thompson and others were running into fame and breaking records. On Sunday night, August 7th Doreen was on the last lap of her earthly race. By this time she was confined to bed. Her family gathered round her when it became obvious that her strength was sinking. She lingered through to the wee hours of Monday morning before she finally crossed over to meet her Lord. Her race was finished. Her conflict was over. Gordon had lost his wife. Sharon, Gillian, Joanne and Laura had said goodbye to a darling mother.

Before Doreen died Gillian had become romantically involved with Eric McCully, the young missionary the family had supported for several years. Eric had now finished his four-year stint with Operation Mobilisation and returned to Northern Ireland to study at Belfast Bible College. During the course of Doreen's illness, Eric and Gillian became engaged to be married when Eric was still in his second year at the Bible College. Gillian's mum did not survive long enough to attend their wedding in December 1984.

After graduation from Bible College Eric and Gillian were accepted into the fellowship of Arab World Ministries which was formerly known as The North Africa Mission. Besides his Christian service Eric discovered and developed latent artistic talents. His fine works on canvas, both in oil and water, are keenly sought after.

God blessed Eric's and Gillian's home in Finaghy with the gift of a beautiful baby daughter whom they named Rachel. In the course of the next few years Simon and Andrew were also born into the McCully home. The sense of loss suffered by a mother's death cannot be reversed by the arrival of the children God gives us. However, the sound and activity of children in a home does augment the happiness of the family.

Eric and Gillian moved house to Banbridge in 1992. Soon they settled into the community and made many new friends at Banbridge Baptist

Church. Gillian enjoyed the family the Lord had given her but felt she would love to have another child. When she became pregnant in 1993 both Eric and she were overjoyed. Her former pregnancies had been quite normal and she looked forward to the arrival of this new offspring.

Although she was a busy mother she was healthy and took appropriate care of herself. It was therefore a great blow to her and Eric when she had to be rushed to hospital in the fourteenth week of her pregnancy. Gillian's pregnancy was harshly terminated by a miscarriage. She was absolutely devastated. Eric was stunned. During the years of affliction when her mother was dying and baby Laura was ill, Gillian had never questioned God's providence and will. In the loss of this little one there was resentment, blame and questioning. "Why did God let this happen. This was our child and we have lost him. Why?"

Slowly Eric and Gillian emerged from the bitterness and trauma of this crisis. They found comfort in the knowledge that the little one they were not able to rear was with granny Crawford in heaven. Unexpectedly there was an upturn in events a few months later. Early in 1994 Gillian discovered she was expecting another child. This child would not be a replacement for the little one who had gone to heaven. He was their child just as much as the two boys and Rachael who played in the garden. Anticipating the arrival of the new baby helped in the recovery from their grief.

As the weeks went by Gillian was prudent and careful not to do anything that might jeopardize the life of the little child she carried. Visits to the antenatal clinic and subsequent scans resulted in positive reports. When she successfully advanced beyond fourteen weeks of her pregnancy she felt more confident that she was not going to lose this baby.

It was with a real sense of satisfaction when at full term, Gillian was taken to Daisy Hill Hospital in Newry for the confinement of her fifth child. All fears were allayed by the caring nursing staff. At the delivery suite there was a short period of labour and Joshua was born quite quickly.

As with most mothers, the pain and discomfort of labour was compensated when Gillian heard the first whimpering cry of her new baby. The nurse wrapped the little purple and wrinkled bundle of new life in a towel.

Eric was at hand to take a first look at his newborn son. He was stunned and struck with horror with what met his eyes. Where there should be a mouth Eric could only see a gaping hole below baby's tiny nose. "What is wrong?" he asked.

The embarrassed doctor said "It seems the little infant has a cleft palate and cleft lip." The doctor apologized that this was not picked up on the scan.

Eric lifted his little son over toward Gillian who had already perceived there was something amiss. With the first sight of her new son there was an initial wave of mixed emotions. Revulsion was accompanied by anger. "Why did God let this happen? Haven't we been through enough?" There was guilt mixed with blame. "Whose fault is it? It isn't mine."

The longer they held the parcel of new life which was their son the more any feeling of abhorrence seemed to drain from Eric and Gillian. Revulsion was soon replaced with spontaneous affection. Tears flowed freely. There was the sense of belonging and owning. "This is our little boy. I love him." said Eric to Gillian. Tears flowed freely as they hugged each other and looked at their little son. They called him Joshua.

Joshua's mum and dad learned that with God there are no accidents, just appointments. Little Joshua underwent remedial surgery and the surgeons made an excellent job of reshaping and repairing his small mouth. Those who meet Joshua today would hardly know that this little boy got off to a difficult start. From his earliest days Eric made Joshua a special feature in many of his oil paintings.

Following this crisis Eric and Gillian thought that they had seen enough of hospitals and doctors during thirteen years of medical emergencies. Sadly there were more to come.

A full programme of meetings and trips to Arab countries kept Eric busy while Gillian worked at Belfast's Royal Victoria Hospital and cared for her four children.   The couple was greatly encouraged by the volume of prayer that surrounded them.   One lady, at the end of a meeting in Ahogill, assured Eric, "I pray for you and your family every day." The McCullys needed these assurances.

In May 1998 Eric was speaking at a church in Kilkeel. During the course of his presentation he felt there was something wrong with his voice. His throat seemed to dry up and he was becoming hoarse. He was forced to terminate his missionary talk prematurely.

Consultation with the family doctor next day led to a visit to a clinic at the same hospital where Gillian worked.   The extensive examinations at the clinic revealed that Eric had a growth on his vocal cords.   He was recommended for a delicate operation to remove the tumour the following month.

After the operation Eric was assured by the surgeon that the growth was a "contact granuloma" – a benign tumor. He was discharged from hospital a few days later with a difficult assignment for a busy house - he was asked to remain silent for two weeks.   Eric happily complied for he knew that as a preacher his voice was vital.   Slowly he regained confidence to engage in limited deputation work. In October, four months after the operation, he went to the Yemen on a special assignment for Arab World Ministries.

It was on Monday evening November 9th 1998 when Eric returned from this trip that Gillian discovered she had an ominous lump on her breast..

Early next morning she consulted her doctor who examined the suspect area and said, "In view of your mother's history I don't like the look of that lump and if you were my daughter I would want you seen to immediately."

The doctor phoned the hospital to seek some priority for Gillian's case.   However, the earliest appointment available through usual channels was two weeks later. Two weeks is a long time when you feel you are sitting on a time bomb. The doctor promised her he would try to find an earlier appointment.

From the doctor's surgery Gillian and Eric went to see Gordon Crawford, Gillian's Dad. He wept when he heard the news. A flood of memories overwhelmed the family. The pattern seemed all too familiar. Even though Gillian tried to console her Dad and assured him that all would be well and the Lord was in control, down inside she was torn apart.

Gillian bravely went on night duty at the Royal Victoria Hospital that same evening. Her growing anxiety became evident to her work colleagues. One nurse kindly offered to try to contact another consultant and bypass the usual red tape and try to accelerate the date for an appointment. This effort was successful and Gillian was delighted to learn her friend was able to secure an appointment for the following day.

Arrangements were made with Gillian's friend Ruth to have the children picked up from school. Eric and his wife travelled to the clinic at the Lagan Valley Hospital. They joined the long line of other patients who needed to be attended. Eventually they were called. Tests and examinations were made. The young parents were asked to return in the afternoon for results.

The intervening hours spent around the proximity of Belfast seemed to drag. Finally they returned to the clinic at the appointed time. Gillian felt apprehension when it became evident they were being kept to the end of the list of those who were to have further discussion with consultant.

The lady consultant in the oncology clinic, besides being very considerate and courteous, was also candid. "The initial biopsy indicates that this tumor is malignant. We need to start you on a radical course of treatment in view of your family history."

Again Eric and Gillian were stunned. Gillian inadvertently exclaimed, "My poor Daddy."

From the hospital Eric and Gillian travelled into Lisburn to break the news to her Dad and stepmother. It only confirmed Gordon's worst fears.

He was broken.   Sharon and Joanne were shattered to hear that their sister had cancer.   Back at Ruth's house the children were bewildered to see their mum and dad upset.   "Why won't mammy come out of the kitchen?" Joshua asked Eric.

For the next four days, Thursday through to Sunday, Gillian cried constantly.   She could not eat or sleep.   She was physically and emotionally drained.   During these days there was a steady stream of visitors to commiserate with the troubled family and the telephone seemed to be red hot with incoming calls.

On Monday morning an inexplicable peace engulfed Gillian's heart and seemed to drown the deep anguish and distress she had experienced in the preceding days.   It was as if she was borne along by an invisible strength.   Gillian remembered what she had heard at church recently, "Often in times of anguish and illness it is difficult for the saint to pray for himself. ·It is then that he will benefit from the prayers of other Christians."

"Christians are praying for us all over the world." This thought touched her deeply and she shared with Eric how the Lord had helped her.

On the following day Eric returned to the voice clinic at the Royal Victoria Hospital for an examination.   While in the Yemen his throat had been giving him trouble.   With the anxiety at the discovery of his wife's illness his throat trouble seemed to be minimized   Another comprehensive examination revealed that the growth on Eric's vocal cords had returned and further surgery would be required.

When our lives are threatened we are caught in rolling waves of repeated emotional reactions: refusal to believe it is true, hostility that questions "Why me? Why this?" depression at the possibility of no hope ahead, bargaining with promises to God if he heals or accepting the Lord's sovereign will.   Eric and Gillian periodically experienced all of these and more.

Since this crisis developed in late 1998 Eric and Gillian have been attending separate hospitals for their respective treatments.   For Gillian the grim course of chemotherapy which was spread over nine months was extremely harrowing. She lost her hair and had to wear a wig which sometimes Joshua whisked off on the most embarrassing occasions. At times she hit the depths of despair. There were weeks when she found it hard to face people in the street or in church. Eric has had three operations on his throat and as I write the growth has returned again.

Through all of this the family, Christian friends and colleagues from Arab World Ministries rallied round to help and encourage Eric and Gillian in many practical ways. Gillian's dad was a tower of strength to the family even though it broke his heart to see his darling daughter suffer in a similar way that his wife Doreen had done almost twenty years earlier. The children were terrific even though at times they were confused with all that was happening. Little Joshua repeatedly assured his mother, "Mammy, I am praying for Jesus to make you better."

Bad news from the doctor has almost been a way of life for Eric and Gillian McCully. The emotions they felt are not abnormal for many who have suffered and suffer still.

Of all the questions that life throws up at us the problem of suffering is probably the most perplexing and difficult. It is not limited to bad news from the doctor. It may follow the break up of a home, the loss of a loved one, financial collapse, unemployment or any of a myriad of problems. Suffering has a way of meeting us in many levels of our lives and the repeated question "Why" frequently looms large for all who are left to pick up the shattered pieces of broken dreams. Dr. Wiersbe wrote a book entitled, "Why do Bad Things Happen to Good People?" I must confess that even after years of ministry I stand as a novice in attempting to address this subject. However, I recognise there are no simple answers. I feel that shallow cliches and trite formulas are an insult to those who suffer.

Sickness and suffering have tracked the whole course of human history since sin entered into the world. From the unjust murder of righteous Abel in Genesis 4 many have struggled with the problem of adversity, pain and suffering. The Old Testament is not silent on the matter but it does not follow a regular pattern. Jacob suffered physically because he disobeyed God whereas Joseph suffered in every way because he obeyed God.

Job is perhaps the most classic example of the mystery of adversity in a godly life. How would we react if like Job, a loving and godly father, we were to suffer complete material, financial and physical collapse and have to look on ten freshly-dug graves of our darling sons and daughters? On top of this Job had to cope with an embittered wife and the criticism and postulating of his so-called friends. The very thought of it all blows our minds yet Job in the midst of all his suffering was able to worship God.

The forty-two chapters of Job present us with different theories about suffering but do not give us the solutions.

Job's friends considered suffering to be God's instrument to punish our sins and chastise His children.

They encouraged Job to confess his faults to God.

Job's wife made the mistake of looking on suffering as an imposition of providence that should make the sufferer bitter against God. She encouraged Job to curse God.

Although Job was a holy man he was also human. He felt pain and heartache. He wrestled to understand what his sufferings meant. At times he thought that God was unkind and uncaring. However, below all his pondering with the mystery of suffering he had this confidence, "Naked came I out of my mother's womb, and naked shall I return thither: the LORD gave, and the LORD hath taken away; blessed be the name of the LORD. In all this Job sinned not, nor charged God foolishly." (Job 1:21,22) and "Though he slay me, yet will I trust in him." Job was able to progress beyond asking the inevitable "Why" of suffering to have the confidence to see Who is in control when we suffer. He said to his wife "What? shall we receive good at the hand of God, and shall we not receive evil?" The Scriptures continue, "In all this did not Job sin with his lips."

WE CAN LEARN THE FOLLOWING LESSONS FROM JOB'S
EXPERIENCE.

(a) Job expressed his confidence in God's sovereign control. Job
     believed that the Lord was supreme and sovereign and all His
     actions are tempered with mercy and love. When we ask the
     question, "Where is God when this tragedy happened?" remember
     He is where He always is. He is right there and in control.
     All of us are vulnerable to suffering. Sickness, disease and death
     could strike any of us at any time. God's children are not exempt and
     some of His choicest servants have suffered very debilitating
     diseases. It is part of the lot we bear since Adam sinned against
     God and sin entered the world. Unless Jesus Christ comes first we
     all must ultimately die, some later than others. The statistics about
     death are staggering, 100% of all people die. The great difference in
     death is circumstance and timing, how and when we die.
     The great message of the Scriptures is that we should be prepared
     for death and prepared to meet God in eternity. That preparation
     has been made for us in Jesus Christ who through His death and
     blood-shedding for us has provided a way to God. He entered
     into death for us and destroyed death and now He lives to provide
     salvation for all who trust in Him.
     As our sovereign Creator He made the body and knows our frailties.
     Every day he gives us the gift of life. He is able to heal but does
     not always heal. Even those who receive healing only receive a
     temporary reprieve for they also will ultimately die.
     On the evening of June 6 1882 George Matheson wrote one of the
     best-loved hymns after a period of mental suffering;

     O Love that wilt not let me go,
     I rest my weary soul in Thee:
     I give Thee back the life I owe,
     That in Thine ocean depths its flow
     May richer, fuller be.

O Light that followest all my way
I yield my flickering torch to Thee:
My heart restores its borrowed ray,
That in Thy sunshine's blaze its day
May brighter, fairer be.

O Joy, that seekest me through pain,
I cannot close my heart to Thee:
I trace the rainbow through the rain,
And feel the promise is not vain
That morn shall tearless be.

O Cross, that liftest up my head,
I dare not ask to fly from Thee:
I lay in dust life's glory dead,
And from the ground there blossoms red
Life that shall endless be.

Eric and Gillian McCully learned that with God there are no accidents, just appointments. God is never taken by surprise nor does the divine Trinity ever take their counsel in emergency. God is always present and in control of every situation.

(b) Job drew strength from God's promises. He had a hope that was steadfast and sure. The southern cape of Africa used to be called the Cape of Tern-pests because of the violent and dangerous storms that menaced sailors. Then a Portuguese navigator discovered a safe passage round the point and gave it the title of Cape of Good Hope. Job, with all his trials, afflictions, sufferings, with death hanging over his head, was filled with good hope: He looked beyond the present suffering and contemplated "For I know that my redeemer liveth, and that he shall stand at the latter day upon the earth: And though after my skin worms destroy this body, yet in my flesh shall I see God: Whom I shall see for myself, and mine eyes shall behold, and not another;" (Job 19:25,26)

(c) Job confessed that he did not understand the mystery of God's way. We often feel we could cope better if only we could understand. Job did not understand but he learned to cope by leaning on the everlasting arms of the Lord. "Behold, I go forward, but he is not there; and backward, but I cannot perceive him: On the left hand, where he doth work, but I cannot behold him: he hideth himself on the right hand, that I cannot see him: But he knoweth the way that I take: when he hath tried me, I shall come forth as gold." (Job 23:8-10)   At the end of his experience he declared. "I know that thou canst do every thing, and that no thought can be withholden from thee. Who is he that hideth counsel without knowledge? therefore have I uttered that I understood not; things too wonderful for me, which I knew not."

It has been said truly, "God is too kind to do any cruel thing to His children,(Romans 8:28-39) too wise to make any mistakes(Mark 7:37) and His ways are too deep to explain the mystery of His will when we suffer." (Romans 11:33)

The Scriptures are replete in encouraging and instructing us in our adversities when it seems that life has dealt us a hard blow. Perhaps no portion is more heartening and helpful than 2 Corinthians 1:1-11. Ten times in eleven verses he uses the word comfort. Paul needed comfort. This is the letter in which he spoke of his thorn in the flesh. In this very chapter he wrote of the trouble that came to them in Asia, "We were pressed out of measure, above strength, insomuch that we despaired even of life:" The suffering to which Paul referred was a compounded set of circumstances. He not only felt pressure from his work and personality clashes with his colleagues but the persecution from the pagans was so intense that they stoned him and left him as dead.

WHAT ENCOURAGEMENT DID HE FIND IN THIS?

(a) By his suffering Paul learned to trust in God. (1:9) God allows
suffering to enter our lives that we may learn to lean more on Him.
The flip side of trusting in God is to learn not to trust in ourselves,
not to lean on our own resources. Often it is by suffering that God
takes away all the props so that there is nothing more to cling to but
God. Later Paul explained that it was the "thorn in the flesh"
that stimulated him to pray and subsequently prove that when he
recognised his weakness then he proved God's strength.

Andre Crouche wrote the hymn that says, "If I never had a problem
I'd never know that God could solve them, I'd never know what faith
in God could do."

(b) By his suffering Paul learned to comfort others. We are most like
our Lord when we are comforting others. He is the God of all
encouragement and to be like Him we should engage in the same
ministry. We are best equipped to comfort others when we have
been there ourselves. The suffering saint can best succour others
who suffer.

(c) By his suffering Paul learned to thank God. Paul reminded his
readers that through perseverance and prayer they were able to give
thanks. "Ye also helping together by prayer for us, that for the gift
bestowed upon us by the means of many persons thanks may be
given by many on our behalf." What began with trouble in Asia
resulted in thanksgiving in Corinth. When we are able to look
beyond the present suffering and instead of asking "Why" we
are able to accept "Who" is in control then our acceptance of His
sovereign rule will lead us in thanksgiving and faith.

Simply trusting every day
Trusting through a stormy way;
Even when my faith is small,
Trusting Jesus, that is all.

Eric and Gillian McCully have not completed their course of treatment at hospitals yet but they do feel they have been in God's school of learning.   Learning to trust when they could not understand and learning to follow when they could not see the way ahead.   At times they felt they did not need these afflictions and most certainly at times they did not want them.   These experiences not only perplexed them, they also have humbled them and made them more dependent on the Lord.

God always meets us in the furnace of our afflictions and walks with us in the flames of our adversity and sufferings.   This is His way of making us more like our Saviour.

Chapter four

Horror In The Home

IT HAD BEEN THE MOST GRIEVOUS OF VIOLATIONS. THE
RECOLLECTION OF THE DEBASING EXPERIENCE HAD SCARRED
Vi's memory and seared her conscience for more than thirty years. Even
though the emotional distress began so long ago it was still vivid to her
alert mind. She is now in her early forties but her soul is still haunted
with the thought of the brutal indignity she suffered within the confines
of her own family.

Vi clutched her handkerchief and dried her tears, with a quivering
tone to her voice she asked, "How could he have done this to me and to
my sisters?" In the presence of a female Christian counsellor Vi told me
her sad story.

She is the fourth of six sisters who were reared in large town in the
North of England. Vi also had four brothers. In comparison to other
children in the surrounding area, they were not the poorest family in the
lower socio-economic community. While Vi's mother worked part-time
in a local "chippy" she also earned some extra cash as a cleaner in several
of the town's posh houses. Her father, formerly a Scottish fisherman,
found employment as a truck driver after he married Vi's mother.

The memories of Vi's childhood and early teenage years still cause her to break out in cold sweat. In her impressionable mind she relives the repeated abuses to which she was subjected as a young girl. In recollection she has more than a suspicion that these abuses began before she was eight years old but the first incident she clearly remembers took place when she was about that age.

It was a hot afternoon when a man from the town bought ice cream for several primary school girls and then offered them a ride in his van. They invited Vi to go with them. He drove them to a picnic area on the shore of a reservoir where people often went to swim. There he provided the young girls with candies. While Vi played at the water's edge she observed that periodically one of the girls went with the man into the van. Vi's unsuspecting mind attached no significance to the incident and nothing happened to her.

However, unknown to this man and the school girls, the owner of the ice cream vehicle became suspicious of the man's behaviour and reported his misgivings to the local police. On the return journey from the reservoir the van in which the man and the young girls travelled was stopped just short of the town by investigating police.

The young girls were taken to the Police Station were they were individually cross examined, first by the police and then by their parents. The police obtained a statement from Vi but her father forbade her to sign the document. He put the 'fear of God' into her when he told her that if she signed the statement she would be taken away from home and put into jail and that would bring shame on the family. At such an impressionable age, Vi was too terrified to sign the statement and was eventually allowed home with her parents.

On arrival home Vi was beaten by her father, forbidden to play with these friends ever again and sent to bed without her dinner. Vi is not aware of what happened to the man involved with the young girls other than being told by a female police officer that he was a child molester. Vi, an eight- year-old innocent, did not understand what a child molester was.

Several days after the police interrogation Vi was going upstairs to her bedroom when her father called her to the door of his bedroom and again began to ask his young daughter what had happened in the van with the stranger at the reservoir. Despite protesting her innocence, questions led to suggestions, and these progressed to exposure and forced intimacies between the father and his eight-year-old daughter. He reasoned, "What you let him do to you, you will let me do as well."

Young Vi was both shocked and terrified. Her father was an ill-tempered man who had often beaten her as well as her brothers and sisters. The children watched in panic and horror when her father on several occasions arrived home drunk and was abusive both in his language and physical force. On more than one occasion Vi was compelled to watch helplessly as her mother bore the brunt of his violence.

Against this background of violence young Vi felt very intimidated when her father threatened her, "If you tell anyone about this I'll kill you."

Although so young, Vi sensed there was something wrong about her father's intimate advances on her. The young girl felt ashamed and guilty. She also was distraught that she could not share what had happened with anyone, not even her mother.

Within a short time after this first abuse that Vi can remember, the father repeated similar sexual abuse with his daughter. When she was nine years old he raped her in an open field not far from the family home. To resist her father Vi was sure it would mean certain death to her. He swore her to silence about his abuses. The young girl had to comply with his bestial and obscene behaviour even though she was emotionally torn up within herself.

Such violent and immoral behaviour continued regularly during the next six years, sometimes in her mother's bed, in the bathroom or the family car. On other occasions he abused and raped her in the fields, at the reservoir while he taught Vi how to swim or in his pigeon loft. Sometimes the aggression took place after a knife had been placed at Vi's throat when she showed any sign of resistance or disapproval. His aggressions were always accompanied by threats of what would happen if she dared tell any one.

This little girl was trapped and powerless. She was caught in an inescapable snare by a man who resembled a gruesome monster more than a caring father. When Vi protested to her father because he hurt her it seemed as though he had a personality change to such an extent that he would later create rows at home and blame Vi for them. Consequently, Vi felt that at times she suffered more from her father's vulgar and psychological abuse compared to what her brothers and sisters bore.

Her world seemed so dark and her life was a bitter nightmare. When other girls spoke of their Daddy's love for them Vi could not imagine that what she experienced is what they meant by love. Vi cannot remember if she ever experienced real love from her parents. She has no recollection of ever sitting on her mother's knee and receiving hugs and kisses or ever being taught nursery rhymes like her nieces and nephews today.

Besides the physical seduction and molestation, the violent father also bad-mouthed his children. He frequently beat them and did degrading things to them. Vi remembers her father arriving home drunk one night and he became so abusive that she with her mother had to lock themselves in Vi's bedroom. Whilst in the bedroom Vi overheard her father ridicule her to the next door neighbour in the street below.

On another occasion he punished Vi's younger brother by putting his head down the toilet and then flushed the water from the cistern over the boy.

Because she was intimidated and put down so much by her father, Vi strove with considerable success to excel academically at school and competitively on the sports field. Outside of her home other children looked up to Vi.

The attempts to suppress the constant feeling of guilt and overwhelming fear finally spurred Vi into action when she was in her mid-teens. She felt she had now developed into being a young woman and should not be subjected to any more of this demeaning and outrageous abuse. "How am I going to stop him? He is very strong. All the family are afraid of him. He is well-respected in the community and no one would believe my word against his." All these thoughts troubled the teenager's distraught mind.

One night Vi's Dad returned for his usual imposition on his daughter. She stood her ground and refused to co-operate. He came at her with his usual vulgarities and threats but she answered, "You put one hand on me and I will go to the police."

At that he froze on the spot. For a moment he stared at her and without any response he advanced again as if she had not spoken. "I mean it. I'll disgrace you in the town," Vi said with a firm tone.

He stopped. He was aware of what would happen to his standing in the town if his behaviour was disclosed. After staring at his daughter with steely and angry eyes he cursed her and left.

Vi was overwhelmed by a sense of relief and yet there was lingering fear. She ran into her bedroom and locked the door. The distraught girl threw herself on top of her bed, buried her head in her hand while her body shook with convulsive weeping. She cried until her head pounded with pain and then finally wept herself to sleep.

For all the years that she remained at home this brutal father never repeated these violations again on Vi although his vulgar and suggestive language continued for a long time and still does occasionally. The physical abuse had ended but she felt chained to her past. Her body was defiled. Her conscience was scarred with guilt. Her teenage years had been stolen by a seductive and impure father. At times she felt she would love to have taken revenge and killed her own father but that would have only complicated her own life more.

The thought of all that had happened remained a secret that she could not share with any one and yet it tormented her continually. To share what had happened to her with others would only degrade and cheapen her life in the estimation of her peer group. How could she?

Bottling up these thoughts resulted in low self-esteem which stole away any confidence of an innocent relationship with any member of the opposite sex. At times Vi had thoughts of self-destruction and on one occasion she ran away from home. Returning home later when she was cold and hungry she discovered that she had not even been missed. The only avenue by which Vi gained any esteem was by proving her physical strength in competitive games or in school exams.

It was some years after this savage abuse had ended that Vi attended evangelistic meetings. As she listened to the gospel preached she began to reason with her heart, "Could the blood of Jesus Christ really cleanse from all sin? When God promised to forgive our sins and cleanse us from all unrighteousness, could that mean there was cleansing for me? It is cleansing and forgiveness that I need most."

Vi did not need to be convinced that she was a sinner. It was the promise of forgiveness and cleansing when we confess our sins to God that encouraged Vi to finally take the all-important step and trust Jesus Christ as her personal Saviour. This happened twenty years ago.

She found the promise to be true. Upon her conversion to Jesus Christ she experienced an inner peace that replaced the torment to which she had been subjected in recent years. It was hard to describe the sense of relief and freedom. It was as if a heavy burden had rolled from her soul or some one had turned the lights on and the darkness had gone. Vi was able to identify greatly with the words of Horatio Spafford,

My sins, O the bliss of this glorious thought,
My sins, not in part but the whole,
Have been nailed to the cross,
And I bear them no more,
Praise the Lord, Praise the Lord O my soul.

Like the woman who washed the feet of our Lord with her tears and whose life had been soiled by sin, the Lord Jesus said of her, "She loved much because she has been forgiven much." This same gratitude was reflected in Vi who loved the Lord for what He had done for her. She wanted to dedicate her life to His service. She trained at Bible School after which she devoted her life's work to a caring ministry and helped in establishing evangelical witness.

Even during her period of Bible School training Vi's visits home were punctuated by lurid and suggestive remarks from her father who persisted in his wicked and immoral talk. The contrast between the atmosphere of the theological school and that which she encountered at home troubled her greatly. There were great struggles in her heart and mind. Satan cast up her participation in the unsavoury behaviour which had been forced on her. He accused and tormented her with the most debasing thoughts. She tried in many ways to free herself from these thoughts.

Vi finally sought help after much soul-searching. She prayed about the matter and while reading her Bible she came on Proverbs 11:14; "Where no counsel is, the people fall: but in the multitude of counsellors there is safety." Many other Bible verses prompted her on to consider asking for help. When she read Proverbs 20:5 she decided it was time to act; "Counsel in the heart of man is like deep water; but a man of understanding will draw it out." Now Vi felt it was time to draw a bucketful of counsel and help from a trained Christian counsellor.

She unburdened all her heart to the same lady Christian counsellor who sat with us while Vi recounted her story. At first she felt greatly relieved by taking this step. She was encouraged when the counsellor assured her she was not responsible for what happened in her past nor could she change what had already taken place.

However, fear and guilt flooded her being when the counsellor suggested that she should confront her father and speak to her mother and sisters about what had happened so many years ago. The counsellor friend wisely indicated that if she did not take steps to do this then her nieces were vulnerable and in danger of a repeat offence as had happened to her.

It took a lot of courage for Vi to face her mother and divulge all that she knew. Vi's mother, was shocked at what she heard but then was even more horrified that Vi had spoken about this matter to a person outside the family.

The process was torturous and difficult but to safeguard her nephews and nieces Vi also confided in her sisters about what she had been subjected to. Tears flowed freely. One after another the sisters admitted they had suffered similar indignities and ill-treatment as Vi. Steps had to be taken to ensure that it would never happen again.

All these measures helped alleviate some of the inner pain that Vi had carried for so long .

Incest and rape are not a recent phenomena nor are they alien to the Scriptures. These immoral and abusive acts are not only stringently prohibited in the Levitical Law (Leviticus 18:6-23; 20:10-17; Deuteronomy22:28,29) but they exacted a very heavy penalty. They still do.

The sad story of Amnon, King David's son, seducing and raping his own sister is a tragic tale. He was so possessed of lust that he deliberately plotted the violation of his sister Tamar even though he knew he was breaking God's law.

David sent home to Tamar, saying, 'Go now to thy brother Amnon's house, and dress him meat.' So Tamar went to her brother Amnon's house; and he was laid down. And she took flour, and kneaded it, and made cakes in his sight, and did bake the cakes. And she took a pan, and poured them out before him; but he refused to eat. And Amnon said, 'Have out all men from me.' And they went out every man from him. And Amnon said unto Tamar, 'Bring the meat into the chamber, that I may eat of thine hand.' And Tamar took the cakes which she had made, and brought them into the chamber to Amnon her brother. And when she had brought them unto him to eat, he took hold of her, and said unto her, 'Come lie with me, my sister.' And she answered him, 'Nay, my brother, do not force me; for no such thing ought to be done in Israel: do not thou this folly. And I, whither shall I cause my shame to go? and as for thee, thou shalt be as one of the fools in Israel. Now therefore, I pray thee, speak unto the king; for he will not withhold me from thee.' Howbeit he would not hearken unto her voice: but, being stronger than she, forced her, and lay with her. (2 Samuel 13: 7-13)

King David did nothing to punish his son for his cruel crime against the King's daughter, but another son, Absalom, waited for his opportunity and avenged his sister by murdering Amnon. This incident in the history of King David's family reminds us that the wages of all sin is death.

The New Testament also enjoins us to moral purity in our relations with the opposite sex. Paul wrote to Timothy to "Flee youthful lusts." (2 Timothy 2:22)   Again he wrote to the Corinthians, "Flee fornication. Every sin that a man doeth is without the body; but he that committeth fornication sinneth against his own body.   What? know ye not that your body is the temple of the Holy Ghost which is in you, which ye have of God, and ye are not your own?   For ye are bought with a price: therefore glorify God in your body, and in your spirit, which are God's." (I Corinthians 6:18-20) Joseph did not live in New Testament times but he knew to flee from sexual immorality when confronted with it.

These inspired words followed in the next chapter after Paul's instructions to the Corinthian Church how to respond to immoral practices among believers in the Church. (I Corinthians 5:1-13) Most Bible commentators agree that the sin which Paul highlights in the Corinthian Church was most likely incest. An unrepentant male believer had been sleeping with his father's wife.

Corinth was a corrupt city and it was likely that incest was prevalent among the pagan Corinthians. That it should be experienced among a Christian family demanded immediate and radical action by the Church. So serious was this sin that Paul instructed that the perpetrator be excommunicated from the Church and delivered unto Satan for the destruction of the body. These measures were irreversible. Discipline and excommunication were designed to help the person to correct his ways. After repentance Paul indicated that an offender is to be restored and accepted by the Church lest Satan have an advantage over him. (See 2 Corinthians 2:5-8)

Until recent years incest was probably the least reported crime in the world even though victims of rape were more forthcoming than in previous years. It is a grievous crime which is more often perpetrated by males on females but not exclusively so. Incest generally creates a sense of hidden shame and guilt whereby the abused victim feels that he or she has done something horribly wrong. The practice of this abuse is destructive both to the child and the family and creates bigger problems for the perpetrator than they can imagine. The perpetrator of incest and sexual abuse robs the victim of any sense of innocence, steals the love of parents and the security of a normal family. The home then resembles more a house of horrors than a haven where love and the Lord reign supreme.

The casualties of incest and rape are not limited to the immediate victims. The perpetrator, be he a rapist or a child molester, is not only a criminal offender but this person needs urgent and radical attention. Because child-molesting, incest and rape are criminal charges the police may become involved. Initially the offender should be removed from further contact with children, especially those within his own family even if it is for a limited period. The person should only be admitted to the family again after there is genuine repentance, professional counselling and obvious reform but he should never again be left alone with children. It is commonly recognised that child-molesters cannot be trusted not to offend again. If he or she remains unrepentant and unreformed his isolation from the family should be maintained.

While this sin and crime is most heinous we must never lose sight that there is forgiveness for all manner of sin, even for the perpetrators of rape and incest. Jesus Christ said, " All manner of sin and blasphemy shall be forgiven unto men:" The promise of forgiveness and pardon holds good for those who are guilty of the worst of crimes when they repent and receive Jesus Christ as Saviour.

The family of a rapist and paedophile are also casualties. The wife and mother may be torn between fear of a violent husband and the defence of her daughter. Where she is unable to give this defence she should seek outside help without delay. Where a wife and mother chooses to ignore what is happening devastating consequences will follow for both her and the rest of the family. Guilt and shame will haunt such a guardian unless they take immediate action.

The wife and mother will also need counselling from a trained person. Where there has been deliberate indifference and complacency whereby the wife has either acquiesced or presided over known incest in a family it will result in inevitable convoluted strains in later family relationships and create grave complexes of culpability, remorse and shame in the individual. This attitude should be reversed immediately, repented of and help sought.

There is mercy and forgiveness also for those who passively ignore incest and rape. The prophet Isaiah wrote, "Come now, and let us reason together, saith the LORD: though your sins be as scarlet, they shall be as white as snow; though they be red like crimson, they shall be as wool." (Isaiah 1:18)

The primary victim in rape and incest is the person such as Vi against whom the foul deed has been executed. Vi needed a lot of reassurance, genuine love and care. It was not a matter that she talked about freely. Indeed apart from her counsellor and family, I was the only outsider to whom she had lifted the lid off her former life to divulge the dark and sad catalogue of her terrible past. It is always important that the victim of abuse should seek reliable help with a trained counsellor or pastor who can help them. Where necessary and when the victim is ready, she should also face the family with the facts of the abuse so that it will not be repeated with other children. There are times when secret matters should not remain secret from those who need to know.

As Vi drew her story to a close she told me of the comfort she had received from the Scriptures. She had read about Tamar in 2 Samuel 13:1-13 and derived much help from the wisdom offered in the book of Proverbs. Vi said, "It is not possible to blot out all the memory of the past, especially when my present poor physical condition is attributed to the sexual and physical abuse forced upon me. Occasionally I have nightmares which flashback to what happened so long ago, but the Lord continues to help me. I am just glad the Lord gave me the courage to speak to a Christian counsellor and then be able to take steps which prevented these aggressions happening to other children."

During the whole time Vi talked we listened almost without interruption. Besides speaking about the criminal aspect of this story, I suggested some guiding principles to help Vi which I have found helpful in counselling other victims of abuse and rape that I have met in my years of ministry.

(a)   I tried to assure Vi that contrary to what she might feel, the seductive behaviour was not her fault. This is often difficult for a victim to accept where the abuse continued over a period of years as was the case with Vi. Often in later years the victim tries to reason why she did not resist. Such rationalizing occurs because the person who was overcome in the offence is now looking at it from an adult's perspective whereas when it happened she was a child who was intimidated and overpowered and viewed it in a different light. Vi freely admitted that she saw her dad as a monster and out of fear, complied with his depraved desires. At eight years of age and through to her early teens she had no power to resist his forced actions. She finally did resist when she considered that she had reached adulthood. Vi was not to blame.

(b)   I also sought to convince Vi that although she had just finished recounting her story to us there was no reason why she should relive the past and spoil her life today. She did not need to live in the past. She had made new affiliations with her sisters who had also suffered similar abuses. They must encourage each other to live their lives without recriminations of the past. Just as worry today cannot change the future so also anxiety and remorse about bygone days cannot change the past.

When Vi became a Christian God took care of her past, her present and her future as is the case with all who know the Saviour. The Christian knows the peace of sins forgiven and the presence of the living Christ within. So great is the transformation in the life of a Christian that for Vi there is now room to forgive those who betrayed her and even forgive the one who used her to satisfy his evil lusts. Our Lord Jesus Christ was also betrayed and on the cross and He forgave those who did the foulest deeds against Him.

(c) Although Vi is a career person and has never married I tried to point out to her that there is no reason why rape and incest should destroy any future relationship and marriage. At her conversion God had made her a new person with a new future. When she was a child she did not have the ability to resist her aggressor. However, now as a Christian woman she has the power to pursue a new life.

Paul wrote to Timothy, "God hath not given us the spirit of fear; but of power, and of love, and of a sound mind."(2 Timothy 1:7) God has given us the strength to do all that He wants us to do. That is what Paul wrote to the Philippians, "I can do all things through Christ which strengtheneth me." (Philippians 4:13) God works in us both to will and to do His good pleasure. If He has a person whom He wants to bring into your life then He will not allow the past to rob you of His plans for your life.

To these suggestions Vi said, "I have memorised several verses that have helped me through all this sad experience and given me strength to overcome; 'The Lord knoweth how to deliver the godly out of temptations, and to reserve the unjust unto the day of judgment to be punished.' (2 Peter 2:9) 'Wherefore let them that suffer according to the will of God commit the keeping of their souls to him in well doing, as unto a faithful Creator.'"

The counsel from these Scriptures cannot be improved upon.

Chapter five

Truth For Tragic Times

IT WAS FIVE O'CLOCK ON SATURDAY MORNING, AUGUST 15TH
1998. ALTHOUGH DAWN HAD JUST BROKEN THE SUN WAS STILL
hidden behind the heavy grey mist which curled and overlaid the folds
and lowlands of West Tyrone. At this early hour William Gibson and his
sons had already grabbed a morsel to eat and were busy herding bullocks
unto a cattle trailer which was hitched to the rear of the family Land
Rover. The men were heading for a cattle mart twenty miles away at
Clogher. Most of the family was still asleep in the farmhouse which was
located on the edge of Beragh.

"What's that smell Ma?" shouted Robert as he loaded up the trailer.
A sweet aroma seemed to hang in the early morning air and he knew it
was not the breakfast for they had already eaten.

"I don't know. It sure doesn't smell like silage or the slurry they were
spraying last night. But sure you get many a smell round the country
here." answered Norah.

The memory of that sweet aroma remains with Norah Gibson as the
first recollection at the beginning of a day the events of which changed

the lives of hundreds of people in West Tyrone and beyond. At ten minutes past three o'clock in the afternoon of a beautiful summer's day, a car bomb, planted by IRA terrorists, exploded in the crowded Market Street in the centre of Omagh. Ironically the street was even more densely packed because police had guided people away from a suspicious car parked near to the Omagh Courthouse, 250 metres further up the street.

The scene in the aftermath of the explosion was indescribable. The massive detonation not only tore the heart out of the town, panic filled Market Street. Masonry, glass and parts of the car scythed through Market Street lacerating and mutilating bodies and causing maximum and mortal injuries. The screams and groans of the injured and dying could barely be heard above the frenzied and hysterical shouts of parents and friends calling out for their children, companions and school mates. These cries, screams and shouts mingled with the cacophony of alarm bells and sirens which were triggered by the blast. Rubble, dust and falling debris from demolished buildings slowly settled on mutilated bodies, dismembered legs, arms, hands and feet that had been ripped from blackened bodies which were caught in the bomb. Empty and battered prams and baby strollers lay toppled over in the middle of the road.

Twenty-eight people (nine children, six men and thirteen women one of whom was pregnant) were murdered and lay dead on Market Street and in its shops. One man died later in hospital. Their lives had been snuffed out by callous and barbaric criminals. Three hundred and sixty-nine people were ferried to hospitals all over Northern Ireland to be treated for severe burns and injuries that would result in loss of limbs and vision. Thousands of people were stunned and shocked. Families were numbed and devastated beyond belief. Loved ones, mothers and fathers, darling sons, daughters, brothers and sisters had been so cruelly and senselessly snatched away in an instant. No warning was given. No time was allowed to say goodbye. Ulster wept in shame and sorrow. This was another day of infamy.

Never to be forgotten scenes were witnessed during the week that followed. Coffin after coffin bearing the dead remains of infant babies and young people, mothers and fathers, husbands and wives, sons and daughters were shouldered to various cemeteries. Mother's wept inconsolably for children who would not return. Pangs of deep grief were felt in homes where empty chairs and empty beds reminded the families of the one who was senselessly stolen from their home.

On Sunday morning, the day after the blast, when the sun rose above County Tyrone's rolling hills, dark clouds of grief and sorrow hung in folds over troubled and broken hearts. Tears blurred the red eyes of those who had agonized through a sleepless night. Shock numbed broken hearts. Families were grieving for the loss of their loved ones. Minds were bewildered. What political or social cause could be advanced with such atrocities? Buildings can be repaired or replaced but those cut off so tragically would not be replaced.

Found under the rubble and debris of Market Street was the body of Esther Gibson, the eldest daughter of William and Norah Gibson's eleven children and the second oldest child among the six boys and five girls. Besides attending primary school in Beragh, a tiny village eight mile from Omagh, Esther seldom missed Sunday School or church in the neighbouring town of Sixmilecross. Like her brothers and sisters she learned the well-known and favourite Bible stories and was taught to memorise the Scriptures. The early instruction in the Scriptures resulted in little Esther trusting the Lord Jesus Christ as Saviour when she was only eight years old

Like many other children from these rural areas Esther progressed from the local primary school to attend Omagh High School. With other children from the area she travelled to Omagh on the School bus each morning and returned home to the farm in the afternoon. While at the High School she made many new friends some of whom shared her Christian faith. Outside school hours Esther helped her parents around the farm and having ten brothers and sisters she often acted as if she was their mother. She was looked up to by her brothers and sisters as the source of all wisdom. Whenever any thing was needed to be known or advice given the recurrent remark was made, "Ask Esther."

Esther graduated from Omagh High School in 1978 and furthered her education at the Omagh College. Afterwards she gained employment as an admissions clerk at the Omagh County Hospital where she remained for three years. From there she moved to Desmond & Sons, the clothing manufacturer at Kelvin Road in Omagh where she became a dispatch clerk at the quality control sector of the factory.

Throughout her school days Esther maintained her stand as an active Christian. This was unashamedly carried on into her working life. Esther was not the flamboyant or vivacious type. Neither was she vocal in the company of strangers. She was quiet and reserved. However, all who knew her also knew that she was a Christian, not just because she told them so, but they also knew the principles by which Esther lived and the Lord to whom she belonged. She was an active foundation member of Sixmilecross Free Presbyterian Church. Besides helping at the Campaigner Youth Club on Saturday evenings, Esther also taught a Sunday School class. She took these responsibilities very seriously and studied hard to present informative and interesting lessons to the boys and girls.

Amazingly, although Esther had a widening circle of friends through her church and work connections she did not become romantically involved with boys until almost twenty years after she had left school. She believed that God had a plan for her life and the margins of her Bible are punctuated with prayers and dates which she neatly wrote alongside certain Bible texts which obviously meant much to her. Against Psalm 102 Esther wrote, "Not my will but Thine be done. Lord remember Esther. 9.15 PM April 10th 1996"

Esther's personal Bible was well-worn. She used a newer Bible to carry to church and teach her Sunday School class but the more used and well-worn Bible she studied at home was a constant source of strength. It is not only covered with red leather, its contents bear the marks of being frequently read and prayed over. Among the many prayers and comments written alongside her favourite Bible verses are some very poignant insights given with her jottings in the book of Esther, the Hebrew Queen whose name she bore. Esther 5:6 reads "And the king said unto Esther at the banquet of wine, What is thy petition? and it shall be granted thee: and what is thy request? even to the half of the kingdom it shall be performed." Beside this verse Esther wrote, "Lord, will you grant me my petition. I humbly pray for a good Christian boyfriend. - May 11th 1993, January 5th 1997, January 12th 1997."

The answer seemingly delayed in coming but when it finally did happen it swept Esther off her feet.

In celebration of Mother's Day Esther accompanied her brothers and sisters in showing their appreciation by treating Mother and Father to a meal at the Silver Birches Hotel in Omagh on Saturday evening, 8th March 1997. Their meal coincided with a Drum Majors' Band Contest which was convened at the same hotel. Taking part in the contest was a nine-year-old niece of Kenneth Hawkes. Following the meal Esther and some of her family stayed on to enjoy the Band Contest and mingled with other friends and visitors.

Kenneth Hawkes remembered, "It was precisely at 10:45 p.m. that evening that I laid eyes on Esther Gibson for the first time and it was love at first sight for both of us. I was two months older than Esther and although we must have been at Omagh High School during the same years, I have no recollection of ever meeting her."

Instead of returning home after the first band session, Esther stayed on for the rest of evening. It was then that she met Kenneth and enjoyed the attention he paid her. The small talk that followed not only helped them learn about each other, it also drew them closer together and from that night they knew they were in love. Kenneth was from Maine, County Tyrone which is about eight miles from Beragh. He was a Christian and belonged to the local Methodist Church. They discovered that they both loved the Lord Jesus and were sure they loved each other.

On the next day Norah Gibson could not have received a more welcome Mother's Day gift than to hear that Esther had a boyfriend. William and Norah and all the Gibson family lost no time in getting to know Kenneth and he was introduced to each of the Gibson clan. They not only learned that he belonged to Mountfield Methodist Church but he worked on the roads for the Department of the Environment and was a piper with the Mountfield Pipe Band.

During the months that followed Kenneth and Esther became so inseparable it seemed they were making up for time they had lost. He became a familiar visitor at the Sixmilecross Free Presbyterian Church with Esther. They enjoyed outings and picnics like most young couple and loved each other's company.

It was on a Sunday evening outing to Castle Archdale, a natural beauty spot in County Fermanagh, that Kenneth proposed marriage to Esther. She had no hesitation in accepting the happy overture. Together they talked and decided to make their engagement official May 31st 1998, which was Kenneth's birthday and planned to marry on 29th July 1999, which was the date of Esther's birthday.

Everything seemed to be idyllic. Kenneth placed a beautiful gold engagement ring with a cluster of fifteen sparkling diamonds on Esther's finger. She wore it with pride and satisfaction. No time was lost in making plans. They enjoyed booking the church, the minister, the reception and cars. Bridesmaids, Bestman and Groomsmen were all invited to share in their happiness. All these plans were completed in a short time.

Kenneth said "We had our rings picked and we were waiting for planning permission to build a house. Esther was kind and loving, the most generous person I have ever known. She loved children. She couldn't wait to start a family. We wanted a boy and a girl." The plans submitted were for a new house they planned to build on a site adjacent to Kenneth's family home at Maine.

During the summer of 1998 Esther had three weeks holidays in August. Instead of going on vacation the happy couple spent their time shopping for their new house. They looked at kitchens, bathroom suites and Aga cooker. Lists were made of the items they would need to purchase. During the three weeks off work Esther saw Kenneth every day and they were radiant when they had the engagement portrait taken at the local photographers.

Soon the three weeks holidays were over and Esther made plans to return to her work in the Quality control sector at Desmond's on Monday August 17th. When she said goodnight to Kenneth on the previous Friday to this date she indicated that there were some items she needed to buy in Omagh on Saturday, including a new skirt. Kenneth arranged to call over to see Esther on Saturday evening. However, neither of them knew that Kenneth's goodnight kiss to Esther would be the last embrace they would share.

Andrew Gibson had gone with his brothers and father to the Clogher Cattle Mart early that Saturday morning but he had left instructions with his oldest sister to take his Vauxhall Corsa car to the car-wash in Omagh while he was at the cattle sale. Esther also needed to withdraw some money from the automatic cash machine at the bank. She left home shortly after 8. 30 a.m. to drive to Omagh and attend to these matters. Esther followed the winding road from Beragh and through Campsie Street on the outskirts of Omagh.

During the short drive she drove behind a red Vauxhall car which also was making its way toward Omagh's town centre. Both cars were caught on camera by a police video observation. Esther did not know that the heavily-laden vehicle in front of her actually transported the lethal bomb that would explode the hopes and dreams of countless families and friends.

After seeing to her business in town Esther returned home. Most of the family had gone about their business. Only Mrs. Gibson and her son Haldane were still at home. Haldane had discovered his talent for oil painting on canvas and spent that Saturday morning indulging in this new found hobby. Esther complimented her young brother on his art work and as was typical, encouraged him and offered a few suggestions on his latest project.

Mrs. Gibson took a short break from her household chores and boiled the kettle. She and Esther sat down in the kitchen and sipped a cup of coffee. Both remarked about the beautiful day, possibly the best day of the summer so far.

"It's a great day for a wedding." said Esther. Her sister Caroline and fiancé had gone to a wedding in Enniskillen. However there was a touch of forlorn hope in Esther's voice. She wished Kenneth and she would be blessed with such beautiful weather for their big day which was now less than a year away.

Esther was jolted out of her wistful thoughts when her mother interjected, "Wouldn't it be great if Caroline and William got a day like that?" Obviously Mrs. Gibson was taking one wedding at a time and there were only seven weeks to October 3rd when Caroline and William Martin planned to tie the knot.

Caroline had invited Esther to be her chief bridesmaid on her big day so mother and daughter engaged in some small talk about the approaching wedding. After the coffee and conversation Esther reached for her books and Bible to prepare for her Sunday School class the following day. She was always conscientious and meticulous about her preparation.

At one o'clock Mrs. Gibson called Esther and Haldane for a plate of Irish stew, a customary dish for Saturdays at the Gibson home and one of Esther's favourites. Haldane was so engrossed in his painting he skipped midday meal.

Following lunch Esther made a list of things to purchase and see to in Omagh. She invited her mother to go with her to town but Mrs. Gibson declined the offer as the men would soon be arriving home from the cattle mart. Esther then asked her mother if there was anything she needed.

"Mother, do you need any flowers for tomorrow?" Esther asked her mother who was busy washing dishes. Norah Gibson was responsible to provide flowers at the Sixmilecross Free Presbyterian Church every Sunday.

"If you see anything special then buy them for me. You know what we like," answered mother from the kitchen.

"I'm going to buy a skirt for work. Is there any thing else you need?" Esther inquired as she finished tabulating her "things to do" list.

"No." was Mrs. Gibson's brief answer.

"I'll be back in an hour Mum," were Esther's last words as she climbed into her green Vauxhall Corsa and sped one hundred and fifty metres down the lane toward the Redergran Road. Those were not only the last words any of the family heard from Esther, it was the last time they would see her.

Esther drove the short distance to Omagh and probably got there at 2.30 p.m.. She parked her car in Dunnes' car park and presumably went into Dunnes to look for a skirt. From there she meandered down Market Street window shopping as she went until she arrived at Nicholl and Shields' shop, a favourite haunt for Saturday afternoon shoppers looking for a bargain.

Having assured her mother she would be back home in an hour, Esther left the shop, still without the skirt she had gone to purchase. She had only taken a few steps between the cars parked in Market Street and was heading towards Dunnes' car park when the fatal bomb, hidden in the boot of a red Vauxhall car, detonated. Instantly Esther was with her Lord. She had gone home to be with Christ.

In the aftermath of the bomb and the horrific scenes that followed police and emergency services rushed to aid the maimed and dying. The first body that Constable Douglas Stewart knelt to give attention to was that of Esther Gibson. It was obvious that she had been quite near to the car which was blown apart. There was nothing he could do for this lovely young woman. Her handbag lay at her side and was half opened. A full bottle of perfume, "Chloe Narcissi," lay at the mouth of the bag. Douglas Stewart opened the bottle and shook half of its contents over Esther's lifeless body and covered it up to be removed to the mortuary.

News of the diabolical atrocity that had been visited on Omagh soon spread near and far. Hundreds of people rushed to the town centre to help and comfort the injured and bereaved. Nurses and doctors voluntarily made their way to five different hospitals to care for the injured and dying. Firemen, electrical engineers and other service personnel descended on Omagh to help without any solicitation.

It was just after three o'clock that William Gibson and his sons were arriving home from Clogher. They had travelled through Ballygawley en route to Beragh and noticed that people were out on the streets. It was obvious that something was wrong. Mrs. Gibson had left Haldane still absorbed in his painting to go into the butcher's shop in Beragh village. While there she heard that there had been a bomb explosion in Omagh. Norah Gibson looked at her watch. It was 3.20 p.m. Immediately she remembered that Esther had gone to Omagh. She said nothing to the bystanders in the shop but quickly made her way home to see if her daughter had arrived at the farm.

As she drove up the lane to the house she was greeted by her husband William and her sons. They said they had heard there was a bomb in Omagh. Mrs. Gibson said she had heard the news in the butcher's shop.

Mrs. Gibson stayed at home on the farm and waited at the phone in the vain hope that Esther would call and relieve all their dreaded fears. The ring of the phone frightened her. It seemed almost like a summons and she froze with fright. When she got the courage to lift the receiver it was Kenneth. He had heard there was an explosion and wanted to know if they were all well. Norah Gibson told Kenneth that Esther had gone to shop in town and had not returned. There was a stunned silence on Kenneth's end of the line and then he said he was going into Omagh to search for Esther.

Esther's Dad, William Gibson, and his son Robert also left immediately for Omagh in pursuit of her.

Kenneth arrived. He was devastated beyond words. William Gibson and his son arrived back to say they had found Esther's car in Dunnes' car park but there was no sign of Esther. One by one in various circumstances the Gibson family not only heard of the awful explosion but that Esther was missing.

Kenneth later said, "I found her car in Dunne's car park and my heart turned over. Her shopping bags were still in the back where she had left them. Her father, brother and I started searching and searching, it seemed to be forever."

Edmund Gibson was on police duty that day but he was detailed to other related work. Obviously some one in the force knew there was involvement for the Gibson family and shielded Edmund from the cruel discovery that his sister was among the victims.

Brothers and sisters gathered at the family home and soon were designated to go to the various hospitals in search of Esther amongst the injured. They travelled to Londonderry, Belfast, Omagh, Enniskillen and Magherafelt inquiring and searching for Esther Gibson. They met many families who were suffering in a similar way as them. People dissolved in floods of tears as they waited anxiously for news of their family members.

Kenneth Hawkes and Esther's sisters went to the Omagh Leisure Centre where the emergency services had set up an information post. Every thirty minutes they read out the names of the injured and indicated which hospital they were taken to. In vain Kenneth waited for Esther's name to be called among the wounded. Periodically the police came to console them and tried to glean some information by which they might identify Esther but no news was forthcoming from the police who were hard-pressed with the sheer volume of work..

The Reverend William Leonard, the family minister at Sixmilecross Free Presbyterian Church, was on holiday in England at that time and was not available to give pastoral care until Sunday when he flew home. However, the Reverend William McCrea had known the family for many years and some of the family suggested that they should contact him to see if he could find out in which hospital Esther might be interned. Mr. Chris Killen, who was spending the weekend in Sixmilecross was the invited preacher at the Free Presbyterian Church. He phoned Mr. McCrea's home in Magherafelt to speak with him only to be told that William had already left for Omagh. In a short while Rev. McCrea arrived at the Gibson farm in Beragh.

The clock struck midnight. Almost nine hours had lapsed since the savage bomb had gone off and there was still no information of the whereabouts of Esther. Finally at 1.30 a.m. the police approached Kenneth, Robert Gibson and two of Esther's sisters who were still keeping vigil at the Leisure Centre. They requested that Kenneth, Robert, Caroline and Elizabeth travel with them to the Lissnally Army Barracks. On arrival Kenneth and Elizabeth, Esther's youngest sister, were invited into the temporary morgue set up at the barracks to identify Esther's lifeless body. It was their loved one. Kenneth and Elizabeth buried themselves in each other's arms and wept.

Still weeping they emerged from the temporary morgue to break the news to Robert and Caroline. They were numbed with grief mingled with anger at the savage barbarity of evil men. Later Kenneth summed up his anguish and grief, "When they murdered Esther, I died with her. I wish I had been with her. I wish I was with her this minute."

Slowly and solemnly they made their way back to the homestead at 3.00 a.m to confirm the worst fears to the family. William McCrea and Chris Killen remained with the family to comfort them and grieve with them until the light of dawn broke next morning. He did not return to Magherafelt until 6.30 on Sunday morning.

During the days that followed sympathy poured in from over the world. Outrage and condemnation was expressed against the perpetrators of the diabolical and ruthless act. However, words and condemnations seemed futile. They could never bring back a sweetheart who was cruelly torn out of Kenneth's arms nor a daughter who was wrenched from the family home.

At her funeral in Sixmilecross Free Presbyterian Church Thursday, August 20th Dr. Ian Paisley said: "Esther Gibson was born with the name of a great Bible Queen, Queen Esther of the Jews. Her young people's work took on a truly queenly nature. And in the soil of this burying ground today we are laying to rest the sacred remains of a young lady who was a queen in every sense of the word."

Sadly Esther's murder in Omagh is only one of a succession of brutal and barbaric atrocities which were exacted upon innocent shoppers, pedestrians and even worshippers in thirty years of terrorist violence and political mayhem in Northern Ireland. In our own congregation at Banbridge Baptist Church David and Ella McCrum carry the tender and cherished memories of their son Alan who at 11 years of age was also killed by shrapnel from another IRA bomb which was planted in the centre of Banbridge on March 15th 1982.

Northern Ireland is not unique in suffering its share of terrible atrocities. We have all been shocked by the multiple murder of the little children at Dunblane Primary School in Scotland, the senseless killings of promising teenagers at the Columbine High School in Denver, the savage mass killing of people at a theme park in Australia and the rampage of murder at a fast food restaurant in California. These are all grim reminders that we live on a fallen planet. There is no doubt about it. All these killings, mutilations and destruction are diabolical deeds. What can we say to these things?

Exactly two weeks before the Omagh bomb, another bomb of similar magnitude was planted by the same terrorist organisation in the heart of Banbridge at three o'clock on a busy Saturday afternoon. As was the case with Omagh, no warning was given. But for the vigilance of police officers and shoppers who alerted the security forces, similar havoc might have been rained on our town as was the design of the evil planners and perpetrators of these wicked devices.

The following morning in Banbridge Baptist Church we read Psalm 37 which was written for times of panic and anxiety.   This Psalm was written by David who as an old man still wrestled with the problem and perplexity of pain and injustice. It is a problem that Job grappled with before David, "Why do the wicked seemingly prosper and the godly face the greatest hardships and tragedies?" Neither David nor Job had any easy answers and they knew no ritualized formula that would quickly dissolve their problems and answer their perplexities.

Amongst the jottings in the margins of Esther Gibson's Bible are some comments written alongside Psalm 37. Above the chapter she neatly wrote, "A Psalm for Stress Management." Her few gleanings in this Psalm serve as reminders to us all of how to cope when we face tragedy.

Psalm 37 was written by David after he had walked with God for many years. I feel that David had learned to view tragedies, injustices and inequities with perspectives that rise above the usual and natural reaction common to most of us. Psalm 37 is a review of lessons David learned in troubled times. David learned to cope with dilemmas by measuring and viewing them in the light of God and eternity.

The same exercise is put to use by Asaph in Psalm 73. He opens the psalm with the familiar complaint and perplexities;

"As for me, my feet were almost gone; my steps had well nigh slipped. For I was envious at the foolish, when I saw the prosperity of the wicked. For there are no bands in their death: but their strength is firm. They are not in trouble as other men; neither are they plagued like other men."

Asaph continued in trying to rationalise his experience of unfairness and inequity in life until he explained,

"When I thought to know this, it was too painful for me; Until I went into the sanctuary of God; then understood I their end" (Psalm 73:16,17)

Only in the sanctuary does God reveal and explain His purpose and plan. It is here that we understand the end from the beginning. It is not what happens in this life here that matters, but in the life hereafter that really counts.

When we view time in the light of eternity, values have a way of changing. What if the righteous suffer? What if the wicked prosper? In eternity all inequities will be balanced, and all wrongs will be made right. In Luke 16:25 Abraham spoke to the rich man and said, "Son, remember that thou in thy lifetime receivedst thy good things, and likewise Lazarus evil things: but now he is comforted, and thou art tormented." This is exactly the same perspective as David encouraged in Psalm 37.

I remember with fondness Hubert Brown from Lisburn. He was a bricklayer who faithfully served the Lord both singing the gospel and using his building skills. I will never forget when Hubert sang;

Not now but in the coming years–
It may be in that better land–
We'll learn the meaning of our tears,
And there some time, we'll understand.

Then trust in God thro' all thy days;
Fear not for He doth hold thy hand;
Tho dark the day, still watch and praise;
Sometime, sometime we'll understand.

It is true that we only see part of the picture here and now we only know a part. We will understand some of the inequities in life and mysteries of divine providence when we arrive in the great eternity. However, how can we handle and cope with these situations now? I have no easy answers either but here are several perspectives I thought of when I looked at Esther Gibson's Bible and shared them with her family.

1. LOOK BEYOND THE TEMPORAL TO THE ETERNAL. –

"Fret not thyself because of evildoers, neither be thou envious against the workers of iniquity. For they shall soon be cut down like the grass, and wither as the green herb." (Psalm 37:1)

We are all so earth-bound and limited in understanding and appreciation of the bigger picture. Death ends nothing. It merely closes the door on our earthly existence and opens the door to the great eternity when the Judge of all the earth will do that which is right. Holding this in view helps us focus on our Lord rather than fret about what is happening at present. Paul writes about this in 2 Corinthians 4:16-18

"For our light affliction, which is but for a moment, worketh for us a far more exceeding and eternal weight of glory; While we look not at the things which are seen, but at the things which are not seen: for the things which are seen are temporal; but the things which are not seen are eternal."

Paul contrasted our afflictions here as being "light" in comparison to the "eternal weight of glory" the godly shall receive in eternity.

According to Paul, Christians should focus on the eternal rather than the temporal as an antidote to fretting over our afflictions here. He confirmed this view of eternity when he wrote to the Romans, "For I reckon that the sufferings of this present time are not worthy to be compared with the glory which shall be revealed in us." Down here in our earth-bound experience we must remember that "Weeping may endure for the night but joy cometh in the morning."

In Psalm 37 Esther Gibson underlined the words, "Fret not..." These two words are repeated three times in the early part of the Psalm. "Fret not thyself because of evildoers, neither be thou envious against the workers of iniquity. For they shall soon be cut down like the grass, and wither as the green herb... Fret not thyself because of him who prospereth in his way, because of the man who bringeth wicked devices to pass...Fret not thyself in any wise to do evil." David's use of the word fret here conveys a sense of worry mingled with envy. (Psalm 37:1, 2, 7, 8)

Fret, envy and worry are futile exercises. Some one said, "Worry is like a ride on a rocking horse – plenty of movement and energy but it doesn't get us anywhere." Worry has a way of destroying our trust in God, paralyses our commitment to God's will, destroys our hope in God's promises and robs us of His promised peace and joy.

Furthermore keep in view that we have a Saviour who is touched with every feeling of our infirmity and knows all about our heartaches. He is the God of all comfort who comforts us. He makes all grace abound to us so that in all things we can have all sufficiency. His strength and grace help us overcome our trials.

2. LOOK BELOW THE SURFACE AND THE EXTERNAL.

As David recalled the prosperity of the wicked and their polluted actions he was able to trace that below the surface there were more sinister forces at work. We can only look on the external but cannot see the internal. We live on a fallen planet with a legacy of murderous acts and horrific barbarities inflicted by evil men.

David not only gave a description of those who practice evil deeds as the wicked, but he also indicated their destiny – the judgement of God. Satan is the agent of darkness and the inspiration of those who perpetrate such atrocities as that visited on Omagh, Banbridge and the Columbine High School. The destiny of the wicked to the final judgement is just as sure as the destiny of the godly to glory and their eternal home.

The author of Psalm 37 was not asking us to jettison legitimate concern for righteousness when bad things happen to good people. Rather he was assuring us that evil doers may escape the sword of justice here but they will face the consequences of their evil deeds before God in the hereafter. As Christians we are not to seek to get even. We are to seek God who will even it all out. We must keep our eyes fixed on Jesus who is the ultimate Judge of the evildoers.

3. LOOK ABOVE THE CIRCUMSTANCES.

"Trust in the Lord and do good..." We are taught to walk by faith and not by sight. Paul taught that "we see through a glass darkly now." We cannot see the whole picture. There is more to life than what lies on the surface and what merely meets the eye. The answer to life's perplexing questions can best be found in the Scriptures which teach us that God is in control even when circumstances do not seem to agree.

David employed such words as "trust," "do good," "delight," "commit," "rest" and "wait" and all of these active verbs are to be placed in the Lord. These words give vision to the Christian in dark times.

Above and beyond our circumstances we are to adopt the trusting lifestyle when we do not understand what God is doing.

Esther was murdered. Her plans for marriage were blown apart. Her life was cut short. However, her life was a complete life in the plan of God. Psalm 139: 16 assures us, "Thine eyes did see my substance, yet being unperfect; and in thy book all my members (days or times) were written, which in continuance were fashioned, when as yet there was none of them." Job also confirmed that God has numbered our days, "Seeing his days are determined, the number of his months are with thee, thou hast appointed his bounds that he cannot pass;" (Job 14:5)

There are many things we find difficult to understand about God's sovereign plan but we know He makes no mistakes. There was never a more unfair death than the death of God's only Son, our Lord Jesus Christ, and yet He not only fulfilled the Father's plan, but by His death He also provided great salvation for sinners.

In John 11 we are told of a little town a few miles outside of Jerusalem by the name of Bethany. The Lord Jesus often stayed in this home where three of His closest friends lived. One day sickness suddenly entered that home. Lazarus grew worse and it was evident that help was needed at once. His two sisters sent a message to the Saviour, "Lord, he whom thou lovest is sick." Significantly they did not ask the Lord to heal their brother nor invite Him to come at once. There was no presumption on what the Lord might do. They merely let the Lord Jesus know what the situation was.

The faith of the two sisters was greatly tested. Lazarus' condition not only worsened, he finally died. Can you imagine what thoughts must have filled Mary's and Martha's hearts. I am convinced that they asked, "Why?"

For several days the Lord delayed with His disciples in a distant town. He then informed them that Lazarus was indeed dead and turning to His disciples He said, "I am glad for your sakes that I was not there, to the intent ye may believe" (John 11:15).

Did you ever consider why the Lord said He was glad that He was not there? Three of His closest friends were involved, and two of them were undergoing terrific sorrow. What a contrast: the Lord was glad while those He loved were sad! Why? The Lord permitted sorrow to come into two lives that He might teach an important lesson to twelve. He permitted disappointment in some for the encouragement of others.

When the Saviour arrived in Bethany Martha said to Him, "Lord, if thou hadst been here, my brother had not died." (John 11:21) "Lord if..." If is a word that hurts when it comes to tragedy. It looks for explanations where no answers are to be found. However, Martha linked the word if to Lord. Lord is the word that heals. He is the Lord who loves us. He is in control of our lives and circumstances. He cares for us every moment. He will comfort us in all our afflictions. As Christians we arrive to a good place when instead of saying "Lord, If..." we are able to drop the If and just say, "Lord."

After Christ had raised Lazarus from the dead and returned him back to his sorrowing sisters, I do not think that Mary and Martha forgot the disappointments they had suffered during those trying days. When they were with the Lord they found that although their disappointments were great, their latter joy was greater.

4. LOOK AROUND FOR THE BLESSINGS.

"Delight thyself also in the Lord and He will give you the desires of your heart." David was encouraging gratitude to enable the saint to endure the sufferings of the righteous. One of the hardest disciplines of the Christian life is to see God's hand in every problem, heartache and disappointment. Too often we can trace His providence only in our joys and blessings but fail to recognise that He can make "all things work together for our good."

Our Saviour said to His disciples, "Are not two sparrows sold for a farthing? and one of them shall not fall on the ground without your

Father. But the very hairs of your head are all numbered. Fear ye not therefore, ye are of more value than many sparrows." Esther Gibson was precious to the Lord during her life here. Her death is also precious to the Lord with whom she now lives in a greater fullness than she ever knew before.

The hearts of the people in Omagh and elsewhere are still raw with pain for the terrible loss they suffered. David views his suffering by rationalizing that better be a partaker of suffering than to be perpetrator of evil deeds and ill-gotten gain. Far better to have a clean hand to handle your troubles and a heart that rests on God's presence than to have a hand that is stained by blood and a mind that gloats in the destruction of others.

Psalm 37 is a contrast between the life and end of a godly person and that of a wicked person. David finishes this song of his old age with these words:

"Wait on the LORD, and keep his way, and he shall exalt thee to inherit the land: when the wicked are cut off, thou shalt see it I have seen the wicked in great power, and spreading himself like a green bay tree. Yet he passed away, and, lo, he was not: yea, I sought him, but he could not be found. Mark the perfect man, and behold the upright: for the end of that man is peace. But the transgressors shall be destroyed together: the end of the wicked shall be cut off. But the salvation of the righteous is of the LORD: he is their strength in the time of trouble. And the LORD shall help them, and deliver them. he shall deliver them from the wicked, and save them, because they trust in him." (Psalm 37:34-40)

God, who keeps the record of all our days, will write the last chapter of our history.

Chapter six

Who Controls Nature?

THERE ARE FEW DRIVES MORE BEAUTIFUL IN THE WORLD THAN NORTHERN IRELAND'S ANTRIM COAST ROAD. EVERY BEND and stretch of the road affords the traveller breathtaking scenes of the Antrim hills and beautiful green glens which sweep down to meet the rugged coast line. Across the waves of blue-green Irish Sea lie the shores of Bonnie Scotland which can be clearly seen on a good day.

So engaging is the scenery that the driver must be careful not to be distracted or engrossed with the vistas on this winding and quite narrow road. One day while travelling on this route I was struck by a warning sign for the motorist just where towering limestone cliffs rose steeply from the side of the road. Large red letters spelt out the warning on the large billboard, "Beware of Falling Rocks."

When I saw this warning I forgot the scenery and paid more attention to the matter in hand. While watching the road and the cliffs I tried to imagine what I would do if rocks began to fall. What could I do? I could not stop them falling or lessen their speed. To try to out-manoeuvre them would be foolish. I concluded there are certain things in life over which we have no control.

At that time I was only thinking of falling rocks on the Antrim Coast Road, but later I thought who can ever control the terror of an earthquake, the destruction of a hurricane, the eruption of a volcano or the direction of a bolt of lightning? With all the wonders of technological advance men have reached in the twenty-first century there are limits to which we can go.   I realised our problem is not how to stop the rocks falling but how do deal with such calamity when it happens.

For Hugh and Ann Brown there were more than rocks falling in Kobe, Japan, on Tuesday, January 17th 1995. They had been missionaries with the Japan Evangelistic Band for ten years and had moved into a fourth floor apartment in downtown Kobe to be convenient to the international school. Their children Ruth, James, Grace and Daniel were able to walk to school everyday freeing up the family transport to allow Hugh to travel to Seishin on the outskirts of Kobe where he was engaged in a church planting ministry.

On the previous night James was anxious about a test he had to face at school the next day. His two sisters and young brother were more free and easy and indulged in a few family games. Unknown to all of them they all had a test to face the next morning but not at school. The children turned into their bunk beds at a respectable hour and Hugh and Ann retired for the night to their bedroom at the opposite end of the apartment.

At precisely 5.40 a.m. next morning Hugh and Ann were rudely awakened out of their sleep by a deep rumbling noise that seemed to reverberate through the building. Sitting upright on the bed Ann did not know if the room was swaying or if her head was spinning but everything seemed to be in motion. Furniture came crashing to the ground. Dishes, glass and all moveable objects could be heard falling and smashing all over the apartment.   Wall tiles in the kitchen popped as they fell off the wall and shattered on the floor. "It's an earthquake," shouted Hugh.

"What about the children," cried Ann. With that Hugh jumped out of bed in the darkness and made his way down the long corridor to the children's bedroom even though the floor under his feet was wobbling with the quake. He pushed open the door to find the children huddled together in the bunk beds. Grace was hysterical with fright. Her brothers and Ruth tried in vain to calm her.

Hugh hugged his children and suggested they all move into the bottom bunks in case the ceiling should come crashing in on top of them. They called for Ann to come. Daylight was still a long way off but when Ann heard the cries of the children she frantically ran barefooted through the kitchen and attempted to open the door to the corridor leading to the children's bedroom. The door was jammed. She pulled hard on it until another shock wave unstuck the door. When it pulled open with relative ease Ann dashed to the children's room disregarding the broken glass that littered the floor. Miraculously she arrived with the rest of the family without not so much as a scrape on her feet.

All six Browns crowded in together on the bottom bunks. Hugh and Ann hugged the children and tried to pacify and comfort Grace who continued to be very upset. They prayed together and Ann reminded the children that many people were praying for them back home in Northern Ireland. Hugh added that best of all, the Lord was with them.

The after-shocks of the earthquake continued to send shivers through the building. Apart from their personal interaction in the bedroom an eerie silence seemed to prevail outside. No sirens sounded. No emergency services could be heard. The telephone line was down. Electric was off. The heavy blackness of the early morning only added to the gloom of the desperate circumstances.

Hugh decided they needed to escape out of the building before it crumbled. Ann reminded him that they needed some extra clothes. January in Japan was extremely cold. To venture outside in night attire would be foolish. However, Ann refused to leave the children. Hugh volunteered to go and look for the coats but how would he find them in the dark? Just with that another shudder ran through the building. This caused drawers to slide open and a cupboard door where toys were stored swung open.

Among the toys that came crashing unto the floor was a novelty flashlight that Daniel had received just a few weeks previous in his Christmas stocking. Amazingly and providentially the impact of the flashlight on the floor switched it on and it caused a beam of light to shine in the room. It was as if the Lord had put the light into their hand.

After fetching some coats and shoes the family wrapped themselves in the warmer clothing and headed out of the apartment. They remembered the old lady who lived alone on the top floor immediately above them. Hugh offered to go up and see that all was well with her but Ann refused to let him go alone so they all climbed the stairs to the lady's apartment. She was obviously frightened but was unscathed. The family then descended the staircase to the street. Even as they went down it seemed that earthquake had left the stairs somewhat askew.

When they reached the pavement they found there were gatherings of families all over the street. Many of the neighbours were too stunned for words. One lady came to them crying asking about her mum who lived above the Browns. They assured the sobbing woman that her mother was safe. Farther along the street older buildings of three and four stories had completely collapsed and there were reports that people were trapped below the heaps of debris. The building which housed the Brown's apartment was one of the least damaged structures in the street. This was probably due to the strict construction laws which allowed for this sort of catastrophe when the apartment block was built twenty years earlier.

The morning air was freezing cold and Hugh suggested that instead of standing around they should walk to where he had parked their car the previous evening. At least it would provide a place where they could shelter from the cold.

For more than half-an-hour the six of them sauntered through the maze of streets towards the Kobe Mission Hall where Hugh had parked the car. All along the route they met groups of people huddled together on the street. Many were weeping and others comforted those who wept. Buildings large and small were either collapsed or damaged. Masonry and rubble were scattered on the roads. Telegraph poles had fallen across roads. There were no rescue services to be seen.

When they arrived at the Mission Hall they were shocked to discover that it was the only building left standing in the street where it was located. Heaps of rubble littered the sites where houses stood on the previous day. However, Hugh could not find his car. Suddenly he remembered he had not left the car there the previous night. He had parked it near to another Evangelical Church which was half-an-hour in the opposite direction from their home. Undoubtedly this lapse of memory was due to the trauma and shock they experienced earlier that morning.

There was no question of Ann allowing Hugh to head off on his own to bring the car. She felt it was of paramount importance that they stayed together because of the confusion that seemed to prevail in the city. All six left immediately in pursuit of the car again. For more than an hour they walked through Kobe's streets. The first signs of dawn which began to steal across the sky revealed even greater horror in the widespread destruction in street after street. For the first time they saw some signs of the emergency services. It was a policeman with a loud hailer. He was serious but it seemed as if his announcement only mocked the severity of the situation. He called, "Does any one need help?"

"Need help?" Hugh and Ann shook their heads. "Where would you begin to help?" For years the Browns and other missionaries of the Japan Evangelistic Band had been striving to help the people in Kobe come to know Jesus Christ as Saviour. Alas, many were too attached and clung to their secular materialism or to their traditions and superstitions to accept the Saviour.

"Who do they turn to in a time like this?" their hearts yearned for the Japanese people.

There was another shock awaiting them when they arrived to where Hugh remembered he had left his car. The Evangelical Church building had not escaped the ravages of the earthquake. It and the surrounding buildings were totally destroyed and Hugh's car was buried in the ruins.

There was nothing they could do as heavy masonry trapped the vehicle. Reluctantly they had to leave the scene and make their way back to their apartment. The acrid smell of burning rubber and wood filled the air. Fires began to ignite as attempts were made centrally at the power stations to reconnect the electric. Hugh and family hurried through the streets in case their apartment was on fire.

Not only was their building not burning but it seemed relatively safe. They decided that while it still was standing they should retrieve some of their belongings from the apartment. Until now they had not eaten, so cereals and bread were provided for the children. Grace was still deeply shocked and refused to eat. Her face gave evidence of the terror that filled her heart. Her sister and two brothers were so glad to see some breakfast. Documents and papers were rescued as well as clothes and valuable items.

At 11.00 a.m. one of the language study students from the Mission's headquarters arrived in a car. The journey from headquarters normally takes one hour but it had taken him over four hours to reach the Browns. They piled all their rescued belongings into the car and soon they were on their way to the outskirts of Kobe.

There was one gasp after another as they surveyed the magnitude of the devastation in downtown Kobe. Modern buildings had collapsed in spite of strict building regulations. Old wooden structures were ablaze. Concrete pillars under bridges had crumbled or toppled, bridges had fallen, highways were blocked and roads had buckled. Slowly and precariously they made their way praying for safety all the way. After five hours they finally arrived with their colleagues Bobby and Tilley Toner and others at the J. E. B. Missionary Home.

There were hugs and tears as they recounted their ordeal. Over a cup of tea they began to enumerate their blessings. Providentially the phone lines were still open and Hugh and Ann were able to assure their families back in Co Antrim of their safety. Although the Browns had escaped injury all the missionaries were aware that tens of thousands of people in Kobe were devastated. Times of prayer at the Mission House mingled with prayers of thanksgiving for protection and with tears of sorrow for those who had not escaped from the grave catastrophe.

The Kobe rescue and emergency services were aided by international rescue teams which flew in to help in the disaster. Stories of miraculous escapes hit the headlines around the world. Concealed below the final statistics which accounted for over six thousand dead and tens of thousands left homeless, were stories of personal and family tragedies. Whole families had been wiped out in seconds on that fateful January morning.

As the Browns flew home to their native Northern Ireland two weeks later they found it hard to believe so much had changed in such a short time. Ann remarked that for the first time in her life she felt safer in the air than on the ground. As if unwinding from the ordeal they relived the whole incident again James reminded them the test that he was supposed to have done that Tuesday morning. "At least I got out of that. That was a blessing." he joked.

Ruth laughed and recalled, "When Daddy burst into the room that morning he came in like a karate expert. His shout frightened us as much as the earthquake."

"It is amazing how the Lord protected that Tuesday morning." said Ann to Hugh.

Hugh and Ann with the children began to recollect on the blessings that accompanied the terrible disaster. Because the earthquake had happened so early in the morning the Browns, like most families, were all together. If it had occurred later in the day then Hugh would have been miles away at Seishin and the children at school. Their panic and dilemma would have been so much greater if they had been separated from each other. Furthermore, most families were all in bed when the earthquake struck and this afforded some protection. If the earthquake had come in the middle of a busy day in Kobe when trains are packed, highways crammed with traffic and the high-rise office blocks filled with workers, then the death toll might have been double.

Soon the children drifted off to sleep and Hugh and Ann settled down for the rest of long-haul flight to London and then on to Belfast.

❖ ❖ ❖

Protection when it comes is a blessing but what about those who are victims in such tragedies? Raimundo was a poor boy who lived in Labrea, an interior town on a tributary of the mighty Amazon River in Brazil. Most of his brothers and sisters were handed out to foster parents and his mother did not even have the means to care for him. The hot climate of the Amazon allowed Raimundo to spend most of his time on the streets of the little interior town where he lived. He skipped school but occasionally he earned a few cruzeiros carrying some freight or running an errand. Generally he picked up a bite to eat here and there from kindly people who took pity on him. At night he rolled into a hammock where, unprotected from malaria-carrying mosquitoes, he slept through to dawn between 5.30 and 6.00 a.m.. With the new day he grabbed a cup of coffee and hit the streets again to live by his wits on a fine balance he had learned to play between poverty and charity.

One afternoon, as is typical in the region, the sunshine which had shimmered with high humidity in the morning was suddenly eclipsed with dark clouds which were laden with rain rushing in from the east. Within minutes of the sun's disappearance, heavy raindrops were forerunners to a sudden cloudburst of torrential rain which drenched the town. Accompanying the heavy rain massive strokes of sheet lightning not only lit up the sky but almost immediately were followed by claps and roars of thunder which indicated the proximity of the lightning storm.

Undeterred and uninhibited by any sense of danger from the lightning Raimundo joined other boys in the heavy rain to be soaked in the downpour. They ran, danced and played in and out of puddles of water around the mango trees on the town's square. For them this was fun time.

It was nature's shower that helped them cool off from the sticky humidity and clean up after sweating through the morning. Suddenly there was an almighty but momentary bright flash of lightning and a simultaneous deafening crack of thunder. Even the boys were stunned by the sudden thunderbolt and ran for cover. Not all the boys made it. Raimundo fell to the ground. The smell of sulphur filled the air. Some onlookers ran out to where the boy lay. In vain they tried to resuscitate Raimundo the street child. Alas, it was too late. Nothing they could do would bring the boy back.

Both of these incidents are more drastic than falling rocks on the Antrim Coast Road but the principle is just the same. In Japan the Brown family experienced a miraculous escape that can only be attributed to divine protection. In the other Raimundo did not escape. Both tragedies are often called "acts of God" but sometimes it seems there is nothing very divine about these calamities.

Overwhelming tragedies occur on our fallen planet. In October 1998 Hurricane Mitch swept through the coastal region of Honduras leaving over twenty thousand people dead in its wake and countless thousands homeless. In December 1999 the worst ever recorded rainfall and subsequent floods washed away thousands of homes on the outskirts of Caracas, Venezuela and buried whole communities under mud slides. An estimated fifty thousand people lost their lives. Earthquakes in Turkey and Greece, volcanoes in the Philippines, Ecuador and the United States hang like Democletion swords threatening to obliterate vast communities.

What hope do we have when surrounded by these potential tragedies and calamities? Psalm 91 is a favourite for many Christians and we often claim the promises of divine protection in this chapter. However, Satan also used promises in this Psalm to tempt our Lord Jesus Christ. Spot them if you can;

"He that dwelleth in the secret place of the most High shall abide under the shadow of the Almighty. I will say of the LORD, He is my refuge and my fortress: my God; in him will I trust. Surely he shall deliver thee from the snare of the fowler, and from the noisome pestilence...Because thou hast made the LORD, which is my refuge, even the most High, thy habitation; There shall no evil befall thee, neither shall any plague come nigh thy dwelling. For he shall give his angels charge over thee, to keep thee in all thy ways. They shall bear thee up in their hands, lest thou dash thy foot against a stone." (Psalm 91:1-3, 9-12)

When we survive tragedies we rightly thank God for His protection. However, we also must recognise that some people are not delivered from catastrophes. This does not necessarily imply that they are not under God's protection. It does affirm that God is sovereign.

Our Saviour was questioned and tested regarding two tragedies that happened in Jerusalem.

"There were present at that season some that told him of the Galilaeans, whose blood Pilate had mingled with their sacrifices. And Jesus answering said unto them, Suppose ye that these Galilaeans were sinners above all the Galilaeans, because they suffered such things? I tell you, Nay: but, except ye repent, ye shall all likewise perish. Or those eighteen, upon whom the tower in Siloam fell, and slew them, think ye that they were sinners above all men that dwelt in Jerusalem? I tell you, Nay: but, except ye repent, ye shall all likewise perish."

Obviously it was thought by some that a group of people who had gone to Jerusalem to offer sacrifices were planning an insurrection against the State. To quell the possible uprising Pilate's soldiers attacked the worshippers when they were in the act of making their offering at the Temple. Their blood mingled with that of the sacrifices they were offering. The other group of eighteen people happened to be in the wrong place at the wrong time when a tower near to the pool of Siloam fell on them. This was another case of falling rocks.

Even in those days people questioned divine providence. "Why did Pilate kill innocent worshippers?" "Why did God allow a tower to fall and kill eighteen people?" These questions posed compounded problems because many reasoned that tragedies proved that certain people were exceedingly sinful and the calamity was therefore a visitation of divine justice. The very disciples were misled by such thinking when they questioned the Saviour about a man who was born blind, "Master, who did sin, this man, or his parents, that he was born blind?"

The reasoning behind this rationale was probably founded in incidents from the Old Testament when God punished certain nations by visiting disasters and calamities upon them. Such was the case when God washed this world around in the greatest flood ever in the days of Noah. Again, God in judgment destroyed the twin cities of Sodom and Gomorrah when he rained fire down upon them.

Various prophecies of the Bible also declare that God will intervene in our world against the ungodly forces which shall invade Israel in tribulation times.

"It shall be at an instant suddenly. Thou shalt be visited of the LORD of hosts with thunder, and with earthquake, and great noise, with storm and tempest, and the flame of devouring fire. And the multitude of all the nations that fight against Ariel, even all that fight against her and her munition, and that distress her, shall be as a dream of a night vision."(Isaiah 29:5-7)

However, our Saviour's emphatic answer to His disciples indicated that suffering and tragedy are not always necessarily directly related to a person's sins or wrongdoing. "Jesus answered, Neither hath this man sinned, nor his parents: but that the works of God should be made manifest in him. I must work the works of him that sent me, while it is day: the night cometh, when no man can work."

Our Lord's answer distinctly suggested that instead of looking at tragedy as punishment we should be looking for the purpose. Affliction sometimes can be God's chastening rod which He uses because He loves us and cares for us. "My son, despise not thou the chastening of the Lord, nor faint when thou art rebuked of him: For whom the Lord loveth he chasteneth, and scourgeth every son whom he receiveth." David thanked God for His affliction. "Before I was afflicted I went astray: but now have I kept thy word... it is good for me that I have been afflicted ; that I might learn thy statutes."

We are not sure what David's affliction might have been, but his reaction to affliction illustrated how we also should respond when adversity strikes us. The natural reaction to suffering is to rebuff and say, "I don't want it." Who does? However, when affliction befalls us it is a hot potato we must handle.

"I don't need it" may be another response. This repudiation of affliction often makes the adversity worse and creates bitterness in the soul. In such bitterness we begin to judge and question the wisdom and goodness of God.

"Lord, what are you teaching me through this experience?" is the response that David must have had for afterward he was able to thank God for the rod of affliction. Such a response produces peace in our hearts in the midst of our afflictions and strengthens our confidence in the Lord.

On the other hand we also recognise that we live in a fallen world where calamity, misadventure and distress are no respecter of persons. As other chapters in this book relate, Christians and their families do not receive preferential treatment when it comes to afflictions and hurt. As long as we are in this world we will be surrounded by dangers some of which we may not even be aware. Our Saviour taught that the sparrow that fell to the ground was precious in our heavenly Father's sight. In spite of how precious the sparrow is to our heavenly Father He does not prevent it falling to the ground.

Eventually all of us will be victims. Some die young and others reach old age but the statistics about death are staggering. One hundred out of every one hundred people will die if Jesus Christ does not return first. If we are not suddenly taken away in an accident or disaster we may fall victim to disease. The real issue is not why death takes some in a disastrous accident or act of God. The real issue is that we must be ready to die whenever that may be or by what means that might happen. Paul said that life was a race to run. For some it may be a hundred metre dash. Some will only finish the race after ten thousand metres. For others it may be a marathon run. However, we will all cross a finishing line some day.

It is not the length of the race that really matters. It is more important what happens after we cross the finishing line. It was this reason our Lord answered those who questioned him about the tragedies in Jerusalem, "I tell you, Nay: but, except ye repent, ye shall all likewise perish."

There are certain conclusions we can make.

I. THE LORD GOD CONTROLS ALL HIS CREATION.

He is in control of the world He created. Through the Bible we come across numerous occasions where God broke through and either interrupted the so-called "laws of nature" or demonstrated His control over them. Earthquakes and fire from heaven vindicated His presence in the days of Elijah.(I Kings 19) God caused darkness at midday and the earth convulsed with earthquakes at the death of the Lord Jesus Christ. (Matthew 27:54) He sent a special earthquake that rocked the prison in Philippi which resulted in the conversion of the jailer.(Acts 16:26-31)

God is still in control of His world today and He rules when storms blow and earthquakes shake our planet. He is in control of your life. Joseph Parker, pastor at London's City Temple, was one of the greatest of English preachers in the nineteenth century who left a legacy of expository sermons. He said, "Affliction always opens the Bible at the right place." After the death of his wife he fell into a period of dispirited melancholy. During those days he seemed to be inconsolable. After he emerged from the dark experience he wrote the hymn, "God holds the key to all unknown and I am glad." The hymn is even better known than his sermons. The last three verses of that hymn are appropriate:

The very dimness of my sight
makes me secure;
for, groping in my misty way,
I feel His hand; I hear Him say,
'My help is sure, My help is sure.'

I cannot read His future plans;
but this I know:
I have the smiling of His face,
and all the refuge of His grace,
while here below, while here below.

Enough: this covers all my wants;
and so I rest!
for what I cannot, He can see,
and in His care I saved shall be,
forever blest, forever blest.

2. GOD CARES FOR HIS CREATURES.

The Lord who controls this world also cares for His creatures. Not only is His creation a demonstration of His goodness but the greatest manifestation of His care was the gift of His only begotten Son, "For God so loved the world, that he gave his only begotten Son, that whosoever believeth in him should not perish, but have everlasting life."(John 3:16) Paul who had previously been opposed to the Lord Jesus Christ had a deep appreciation for that love when he wrote, "He that spared not his own Son, but delivered him up for us all, how shall he not with him also freely give us all things?"

According to Paul there was no limitation put on the price God paid to save sinners from their sins. He really cares for us.

3. GOD IS ABLE TO COMFORT US IN ALL OUR DIFFICULTIES.

When Hugh and Ann Brown escaped from the destruction of the Kobe earthquake they were greatly comforted by the same Psalm that comforted Martin Luther in his trials five hundred years ago and has brought comfort to thousands since – Psalm 46.

God is our refuge and strength, a very present help in trouble. Therefore will not we fear, though the earth be removed, and though the mountains be carried into the midst of the sea; Though the waters thereof roar and be troubled, though the mountains shake with the swelling thereof. Selah. (Psalm 46:1-3)

God is not absent in our troubles. He is always present and always available to help us. He is our refuge to hide us, our strength to hold us and He is always present to help us even when the unmovable things of life begin to shift. Based on this confidence the Psalmist was able to say "Therefore we will not fear, though the earth be removed..."

The earth moved that Tuesday morning in Kobe.

Chapter seven

Empty Arms, Breaking Hearts

TREVOR AND ESTHER GILLANDERS WERE TEENAGE SWEETHEARTS. AFTER THEY WERE MARRIED GOD BLESSED THEIR HOME WITH A healthy baby boy, Darren, in April 1979. Two years later Esther announced to Trevor that she was expecting their second child. Sadly, they recognised little about God's blessings on their home for they were a happy-go–lucky couple enjoying their little boy and endeavouring to get on in life.

Trevor was a baker in Monaghan and although the wages were not great at the time, he and Esther scraped enough money together to put a deposit on a house. Payment of a mortgage and running an old car limited their budget but Trevor still enjoyed his wine at the weekends and whenever he could afford it.

With the expectation of another child the young couple planned ahead with anticipation. Perhaps Trevor was the more carefree of the two and he tried to dismiss any apprehensions that Esther expressed about the well-being of their second child. She had a nagging premonition that this little one would be handicapped in some way but Trevor was always positive and deftly tried to divert Esther's thoughts from such a mishap. Visits to the doctor did not give any cause for concern in this respect but Esther could not be convinced otherwise.

In August 1981 Esther was admitted to the local maternity unit for the imminent arrival of the baby. Trevor spent some time with her but the prolonged labour was a poignant harbinger that all was not well. The medical staff advised Trevor to go home and if there was any news they would send for him.

Baby Raymond Gillanders was finally born at 4.30 in the morning, a full twenty-four hours after Esther had gone into labour. Trevor was not present and just at the moment that little Raymond was delivered Esther turned to the midwife and said, "I don't want to see the baby for I know he is a Down's Syndrome baby."

The midwife was astounded. "How did you know?" asked the midwife who was obviously embarrassed.

The very reply confirmed Esther's worst fears. "I knew it all along," said Esther through her tears.

The midwives complied with Esther's request and little Raymond was whisked off to the newly-born baby unit. A kind nurse tried to comfort Esther and sympathetically said, "God looked down from heaven for a home for this little baby and sent him to you and Trevor."

Trevor was wakened out of his sleep early morning to learn that the hospital had been trying to contact him. He was not staying at the same address as the number left at the maternity unit. He phoned through immediately and was told to come to the hospital as there were complications and his wife was very distressed. He went straight to the hospital to be at Esther's side.

Esther was transferred to a semi-private ward separated from the other mothers. After consoling his wife and listening to all that had transpired, Trevor decided to go to the nursery and see his new son. Esther was unable to accompany him because of the treatment she was receiving.

Soon he returned and with a smile on his face to encourage his wife, he said, "Esther I don't see anything wrong with him. He looks normal and he is our wee son." He hugged his wife and together they cried.

Later in the morning Trevor had to leave to attend to matters in Monaghan and Esther was left alone. As Esther lay on her bed thinking on all that had happened she had a tremendous urge to go to the nursery and see Raymond. Slowly she made her way toward the nursery and without anyone indicating which baby was hers, as if by some inexplicable instinct she went straight to where her little baby lay in an incubator. She looked at the little hands and feet, the cute little face with button mouth and tiny eyes.

Just the then the nurse on duty arrived and encouraged Esther to open the incubator and touch her boy. In those moments when their hands touched and Esther gazed on her tiny baby the bond that fused between Esther and little Raymond was almost palpable.

"How did I refuse to look at him when he was born?" Esther's remorse caused her to sob deeply. "How will he ever forgive me?" she said to the kind nurse who held her hand. The nurse apologized that she was not able to be at Esther's side when Raymond was born. She cried with Esther until she had to leave to look for tissues.

In the solitude of her private ward Esther mused on all that had happened. She was surprised that her early premonition during pregnancy had not prepared her for the shock of Raymond's handicap. The inevitable questions flooded her mind. How did it happen? Why did it happen to us? How will we cope? What will Darren think of his baby brother? Darren...? I must have a photo of Darren with me." These thoughts tortured Esther's mind. She was only alone for a few hours but it seemed like an eternity.

When Trevor left the hospital he passed by the home of a neigbour with whom he had no previous contact. Violet had a son who was Down's Syndrome. Just the day before Raymond was born Esther had met Violet in Monaghan and in course of small talk asked, "How is Mark?" Violet had been touched by Esther's inquiry. Trevor broke the news to Violet for he felt she could identify with how his wife was feeling.

It was Violet's arrival at the hospital that broke the loneliness in Esther's private ward. She had brought a present for Raymond - a small outfit for a new-born baby boy. Esther was very touched by her kindness. It was the first positive token she had received since the arrival of her little son. Violet did not speak in any sort of pitiful way about Raymond's condition. She told Esther of how well Mark was doing and how he was developing. That visit forged a strong bond between the two mothers.

The paediatrician told Trevor and Esther that Raymond's general health seemed to be satisfactory in spite of the Down's Syndrome, however, they would like him to remain in hospital for a few days while she could go home.

It came as a complete shock when suddenly Esther got word to say that Raymond had a heart condition and needed hospitalization in Drogheda. Drogheda? That was fifty-four miles away. Esther was told that no other hospital would accept the child because he had not been baptized.

Esther and Trevor also put great emphasis on christening a baby and because they felt Raymond was near death they called for the minister to baptize their son. The Rev. David Hillen assured Trevor and Esther that infant baptism was not necessary.

For the next six weeks Trevor and Esther went through their worst nightmare. They travelled one hundred and eight miles to and from Drogheda to be with baby Raymond every day. Trevor worked long and unsociable hours at the bakery and did not arrive home until after six o'clock most evenings. As soon as he got home they left Darren with their family and headed down the road to Drogheda.

At the hospital their precious little treasure lay in an incubator. Dressings covered his little eyes, bandages were wrapped around his tiny hands, leads were attached to vital areas around the heart, a subcutaneous drip punctured the top of his small head and tubes were used to feed him. He needed round the clock attention. Just to drip-feed him was a full days work for it took two hours to give him five millimeters and by the time that was administered the next feed was due.

Downs syndrome was no longer of any significance. Little Raymond was fighting for his life and it was breaking Mummy and Daddy's heart. The medical staff explained that Raymond had an enlarged heart and enlarged liver.

Raymond's condition improved sufficiently for Trevor and Esther to take him home to Monaghan. Now their son was with them the doting parents loved him and gave him the maximum attention.   Having to care for Raymond was no ordeal for Esther. She did that with great satisfaction. However, she was frightened that she would not be able to administer the medicine in the proper way and at the right time. It seemed as if the hospital had sent enough medicine to fill a chemist's shelf.

Darren came to the rescue. He was careful not to let his baby brother cry. He learned what colour of medicine came in what order and at what time and made sure his Mummy remembered them.

For the next seventeen months Trevor's and Esther's life revolved around Raymond's schedule. The little child was sickly throughout those months. Seventeen times he developed pneumonia – one every month. Five times he went into heart failure and had to be rushed to hospital on every occasion. Their little baby just lived on the brink of death.

During all this time they developed a growing relationship with little Raymond.   They loved him and cuddled him and he seemed to reciprocate that love. He had a cute smile and a twinkle in his little eyes that stole their hearts. Between visits to the hospital Darren kept his little brother amused and soon introduced him how to play with the famous Fisher Price early learning toys. With the passing of months Raymond learned to crawl. He rolled over and over to get from the living room to the kitchen.

Trevor's wages were not great. When they had to travel to Drogheda every day for a week which happened at regular intervals, it took most of Trevor's wages just to pay for petrol. It was difficult to keep up with the mortgage and still provide for the other necessities of life. They could not afford central heating so they installed an infra-red lamp over Raymond's cot to keep him warm and covered his head to protect him from the lamp. Trevor and Esther slept at alternate sides of the bed each night to take care of Raymond when he wakened in the wee hours of the morning. They soon developed the ability to sleep and listen at the same time.

Some friends and family tried to support Trevor and Esther in their demanding timetable. Raymond even developed a keen tie with a baby sitter who often came to help Esther at home. Friends in the United States unknown to Trevor and Esther, meant well when they heard of Raymond's birth and sent a Bible text that said, "And we know that all things work together for good to them that love God, to them who are the called according to His purpose." They also kindly sent Dale Evan's little book, "Angel Unawares" which tells the story of how she and her husband, Roy Rogers, coped with the birth of their handicapped child.

During all these months of Raymond's illness Trevor and Esther discussed death regularly. Raymond's condition helped them sort out priorities in their lives. They recognised that it was inevitable that Raymond would not survive too long. The hospital had given them hope that he would live for five or six years. However, they were not Christians. Only occasionally did they attend the Presbyterian Church to which they belonged. In their ignorance and in a vain attempt to help Raymond they listened to old wives' tales and even indulged in asking people to charm their child.

It came to the attention of Trevor and Esther that Rev. Sam Workman was conducting special meetings in the Hillgrove Hotel in Monaghan. They had heard that Mr. Workman frequently prayed with the sick and these frequently resulted in some remarkable healings. One night the anxious couple made their way to the hotel a good while before the meetings started in the hope of meeting the preacher and asking him to pray for their son. Mr. Workman was in a prayer meeting when they arrived but on hearing of the couple he came out to meet them.

They shared with God's servant the history and condition of their infant son. That night Esther felt that the Rev. Workman prayed a strange prayer which went something like, "Lord if it is your will to heal baby

Raymond then touch him but if it is not your will give the parents grace
and strength and help them to come to know the Lord Jesus."

Trevor and Esther stayed on for the meeting. They do not remember
any other part of the sermon other than the preacher speaking plainly and
directly to the people, "You farmers know that the only way to get the wily
old ewe to go into a wagon is to grab the lamb and carry it in first. Once
the ewe sees you farmers carrying the lamb then they follow after you.
The Lord is the Good Shepherd and sometimes He takes our little lambs
so that we might follow Him. "

Esther listened to what Mr. Workman said but she felt that if the good
Shepherd was to take her little lamb she could not follow the Shepherd.

One morning early in the New Year Esther was startled when she went
to lift Raymond from his cot. His mouth and face were covered in blood.
This had happened before when the little boy went into heart failure.
Darren had already gone to school and Trevor was at the bakery. They
had no telephone at home. Esther washed her baby and wrapped him in
blankets. She placed him in the push chair and hurriedly made her way
the two miles to town where she picked up Darren and then went to the
doctor's surgery. Periodically she had to stop and wipe Raymond's mouth
each time he coughed up bright red blood.

The doctor said Raymond would have to go to Drogheda immediately.
The fifty-four miles to the hospital seemed to never end. In the car
Raymond, pale and pathetic, lay limp in Esther's arms. Little pink spots
had appeared on his face. Esther was not a praying person but she prayed
all the way to the hospital. In the back of her mind was the thought that
the oxygen tent will solve this. He has pulled through so many times and
the doctors had suggested to them that Raymond might live for five or six
years.

On arrival at the hospital Raymond was rushed into the ward. Some
discussion took place as to what was the cause of this latest crisis. Much
against Trevor's and Esther's wishes it was decided to do a lumber
puncture on their little son. The thought of it hurt them deeply. They
remained at the hospital until almost 1.00 a.m. Trevor had to start work

at 6.30 a.m. so they felt they should travel back home. Before leaving they went in to see Raymond lying in his familiar surrounding – an oxygen tent with tubes and leads all around him. They lifted their hand to the side of the tent and Raymond, as if to reassure his Mummy and Daddy, placed his tiny hand on the inside of the plastic to meet theirs. Their hearts were melted.

Reluctantly they tore themselves from their son's side and made for the car. The journey home was like a bad dream. Not only were their hearts broken and both wept for their baby but they ran out of petrol and their car ground to a halt at the side of the road. To make matters worse, they had no money. Esther had to help Trevor push the car to a petrol station which fortuitously was not too far away. Explaining their circumstances the proprietor allowed them to have some petrol to pay on another occasion. They eventually arrived home after 3.00 a.m.

Neither of them could sleep. Esther recalled that she noticed just before Christmas Raymond did not have the strength to roll over or crawl his way to the kitchen. Now she knew that her little son must have been tired and had lost his strength. Trevor could not forget that on the previous night little Raymond had looked over at him and gave a reassuring smile as if to comfort his parents prior to this ordeal.

They phoned the hospital every hour. Finally Trevor had to leave home for the bakery. Esther counted the hours for her husband to arrive home so that they could travel to Drogheda again. In the early evening a neighbour received a call requesting her to contact Trevor and Esther and tell them to go the hospital immediately.

Esther was distressed. She phoned the bakery to ask Trevor to come immediately but he had already left. Just after Trevor arrived his boss came to their home. He was distraught. Although he was not a religious man in any way the owner of the bakery offered to pray with Esther. She felt it was too late for that. She just wanted to get to the hospital.

The journey to Drogheda was reckless beyond belief. Esther's prayers alternated between keeping them safe on the road and keeping Raymond alive until they got there.

When they arrived they went straight into the ward where Raymond had been. The compassionate nurse assigned to meet them had missed the couple. When they got to where Raymond was the nurse was at his side. She explained to them that little Raymond had put up a brave fight but as he fought his heart gave up and he suddenly passed away. It was then that they phoned which meant he had been dead for almost two hours.

Trevor and Esther were stunned. "Why? Where is God in all of this? Our little boy died alone."

Esther dissolved in tears. She lifted little Raymond's tiny hand. It was growing cold and instinctively Esther began to rub it in a vain attempt to warm him up. Tears flowed freely. The nurse on duty requested that Esther should not cry in the ward as it would upset other patients. In her heart Esther resented the nurse's request. Why should I keep quiet? I need to cry. My boy is dead. She tried to restrain the impulse to pick Raymond up in her arms and run off with him.

On arrival back in Monaghan the house was crowded with people. Family, friends, and unfamiliar faces had come to sympathise with the young couple but they were too dazed to relate to anyone. They hugged Darren who came running to them saying "Mummy and Daddy, Raymond is in heaven."

Esther went to the bedroom and again dissolved in deep sobs when she saw the empty cot. The impact of empty arms, and empty house, empty hearts and the now silent voice were just too much to bear. Instinctively Esther fixed the sheets and blankets as she had done all other nights for her son. Only the reassuring comments of Darren seemed to get through to Esther, "Mammy, Raymond is with Jesus in heaven."

At the funeral service Rev. David Hillen graciously addressed the congregation from Mark 10:14, "Suffer the little children to come unto me..." He posed probable questions that parents ask in times of bereavement. "You can know where he has gone," said the minister. He then quoted the Scriptures "A little child shall lead them..." Trevor and

Yvonne did not know the meaning or significance of these words at that time.

Trevor and Esther requested that they sing a hymn she had heard at Rev. Workman's meeting some months earlier:

I hear Thy welcome voice,
That calls me now to Thee,
For cleansing in the precious blood
That flowed on Calvary

As the large congregation sang the refrain three times Esther could see Raymond. The Good Shepherd had taken Him. Stirred with grief and emotion she sang with them.

I am coming Lord,
Coming now to Thee
Wash me cleanse me in the blood,
That flowed on Calvary.

However, Esther's heart was fast closed against the Lord. She had no sense of repentance.

During the months that followed Raymond's death Trevor and Esther rode an emotional roller coaster. In September 1983 they fostered six-month-old Nicola. She was not a replacement for Raymond but she did help the family and stayed with them for six years.

Faithfully and patiently Rev. David Hillen visited their home and counselled them in their grief. Esther's father was diagnosed with cancer six months after Raymond's death and passed away seven months later.

During her father's illness Esther and Trevor had lost all interest in their former pleasures in the world. They stopped smoking and even gave up their alcoholic drinks. They became more aware of their own mortality and the need of God in their lives. Esther became very concerned to know if her father was a Christian. It seemed as if an inner voice rebuked her, "What right have you to inquire about others when your own heart is not right with God?"

David Hillen counselled the couple and witnessed to them about salvation. However they learned that there was a price to pay. They would have to confess their sin and turn their back on their former ways. Spiritual matters often entered their conversation at home and they felt the step to conversion was imminent.

In November 1984 Esther was attending a course in Navan while Trevor stayed at home with Darren and Nicola. He spent the evening listening to records and especially the mellow tones of Jim Reeves sing "I'd rather have Jesus than silver or gold." and "Have thine own way Lord." Repeatedly he put the arm of the record player back to listen one more time to the words of that hymn. Trevor could resist no longer and even though Esther was not at home, he knelt at the side of the settee. He did not know what he should do. In his heart he knew he wanted to get right with God. Just in his own words and as best he knew how he asked the Lord Jesus Christ to become his Saviour.

Immediately he felt things were different. He could hardly wait for Esther to arrive to tell her the news. When he did tell her she became quite cross and was angry at Trevor taking this step without including her. For the next few days Trevor was as happy as Esther was miserable. Unaware of the misery Esther was passing through Trevor either sang or whistled some hymns and choruses which only exacerbated Esther's wretchedness.

Esther reasoned within her own heart what it would cost her to be a Christian. She had already suffered the loss of her darling son. Suddenly the thought struck her as if God was reasoning with her, "Cost you? Why I had only one Son and I gave Him for you." The thought crushed Esther who sank to her knees at the side of her bed, repented of her sin and received the Lord Jesus Christ as her Saviour.

She received assurance immediately and her life seemed changed on the inside. However, she dreaded telling people for she feared their ridicule. Trevor was unabashed and told everyone. For six months Esther told no one other than Trevor that she was a Christian. When she finally did confess Jesus Christ as Saviour to her sister-in-law, a great peace flooded her heart.

Trevor and Esther Gillanders have come a long way since then. They serve as evangelists with the Faith Mission and God has richly blessed their work and witness. Today they have two boys, Darren and Gregory. Raymond is still very much part of their lives for he helped shape them and prepare them for all that God had purposed in their lives.

❖ ❖ ❖

One of the hardest things I have had to face in forty years of pastoral and missionary service has been the heart-rending task of comforting grieving parents during the terminal illness and subsequent death of their children or trying to bring succour to parents who have lost children in miscarriage. Such cases are too numerous to mention.

What consolation can be brought to the hearts of those who have lost children? Humanly speaking a child's early death seems so wrong and so premature. It is hard for adults to bury their parents but that is to be expected. For parents to lay the remains of their little one in the grave is heart-rending. How can life be faced without seeing your children grow up? These questions painfully well up in the minds of those who have passed through this painful experience.

As Gordon and Alison Chesney know, there is no sorrow quite so heartbreaking as that of the death of a little child. They were expecting the arrival of their first-born but again, after protracted labour, little Joel was born with congenital abnormalities of his heart. They waited vigilantly at his bedside in the Intensive Care Unit of the Royal Victoria Hospital in Belfast for a full week, hoping all the time and soliciting the prayers of godly people, that their little treasure would be spared. Sadly he was not.

Exactly one week after he was born the surgeon sent word to the waiting parents to say that their baby Joel had died as he was being prepared for the operation to correct the abnormalities. Two hours later Gordon and Alison were told that there was a mistake and their little boy had not died. He was still breathing. Hopes were raised. Has God performed a miracle? Alas, their raised hopes were dashed again when little Joel slept away in his father's arms a few hours later.

When a child dies tears fill the eyes, pain breaks the heart, the silent home and grieving parents bemoan the empty arms and empty cot. The image of the smiling face, the deep dimples, the little nose and shining eyes of that little one are permanently etched on the hearts and minds of the grieving parents. The semblance of the infant will be so vivid at the darkest hours of night for years to come. The memory of the toddler's gibbering will linger with the parents through many silent hours of life. Other children may be reared and loved in the home but no other child will fill the empty arms or replace the little one who departed for heaven.

To all such grieving parents God gives special promises in His Word for He is "the Father of all mercies and the God of all comfort." (2 Corinthians 1:3) This comfort may be found in the tender and compassionate assurances which are discovered in His Word.

I like the story told by Dr. Vernon Magee of a little girl who travelled for a long distance with her parents in a sleeper train. It was the first time for Mary to travel on a train and she was rather frightened. To alleviate those fears her father and mother climbed into an upper berth, and they tucked her into the lower berth.

The little daughter, down below by herself, soon began to whimper. The mother reached down to calm her and said to her "Darling Mary, God is with us, don't be afraid. He will take care of us."

Mary was quiet for a few moments. Then she asked, "Daddy, are you up there?"

Father reached out and said, "Yes, I'm up here."

A few minutes later she asked again, "Mummy, are you up there?"

Her Mummy reached down and said, "Yes, I'm here."

A very exhausted passenger who was in an upper berth across the aisle interrupted, "Little girl, we're all here. Your mama is here, your daddy is here, your brother is here, your sister is here, your aunt is here, your uncle is here, your cousins are here, we're all here. Let's go to sleep!"

There was silence for another few moments, but the stillness was broken by the soft voice of the little girl inquiring, "Mummy, was that God?"

God was very real to her. She thought He was right there with Mummy and Daddy. We all need to be assured of the reality of God in our sorrow and to know that He is the God of all comfort.

The people of Israel, fresh out of Egypt after the miraculous opening of the Red Sea, travelled for three days without water. When they arrived at Marah they discovered that the water in the well was bitter. The people seemed inconsolable until Moses cut down a tree and cast it into the bitter waters. Instantly and miraculously the waters were made sweet. (Exodus 15:15-22)

Into the bitter waters of human experience God cast the healing of another tree. It was on the cross that Jesus Christ died for us and rose again from the tomb. He has given us blessed hope that can take the gloom from the tomb and brighten our darkest hour with His comfort. I would not presume that there is no sting in the heavy heart that grieves. However, the hope that the Saviour gives us allows for the tears but also wipes them away.

What is the comfort He brings to us?

Jesus loves and cares for little children. While on earth the Lord Jesus consistently expressed His love and esteem for little children. Many of His miracles involved boys and girls. He took the children upon His knee and prayed for them and blessed them. (Matthew 19:13-15) The Lord Jesus set a child in the midst of religious adults and admonished them to become like little children. (Matthew 19:2-4) Our Saviour wept at the death of Lazarus also He wept in sympathy for the children of Jerusalem. "O Jerusalem, Jerusalem, thou that killest the prophets, and stonest them which are sent unto thee, how often would I have gathered thy children together, even as a hen gathereth her chickens under her wings, and ye would not!"

He loves them still and is touched with every pang of pain which grieving parents feel.

Every life is a complete life. A race for some may be a hundred metre dash while for others it can be longer. Some flowers bloom for weeks while others flourish but for a day. We measure life by the span of time we know and any thing short of "a good age" we look upon as a premature death. God measures a life by eternity. Even a little child or a miscarried baby who did no work nor developed any sort of character on earth has an immortal spirit and living soul. The completeness of that child is realised in eternity.

Moreover, the influence of your little one lives on with you for the rest of your life. In the Scriptures we read that Methuselah, the oldest man that ever lived, made a greater impact on his father at his birth than He did in his the rest of his life. Genesis 5:21 informs us that when Methuselah was born his father Enoch began to walk with God. We are not aware what Enoch did prior to his son's arrival but the birth of Enoch's first child motivated him to walk with God. If baby Methuselah had died as an infant he would have already accomplished a great purpose.

Your departed child is with the Saviour. King David had two sons who died. He loved them greatly and deeply grieved over their death. One was Bathsheba's child who died a short time after birth. The measure of David's grief can be understood by his attitude and action at the death of the little one.

David therefore besought God for the child; and David fasted, and went in, and lay all night upon the earth. And the elders of his house arose, and went to him, to raise him up from the earth: but he would not, neither did he eat bread with them.

And it came to pass on the seventh day, that the child died. And the servants of David feared to tell him that the child was dead: for they said,

Behold, while the child was yet alive, we spake unto him, and he would not hearken unto our voice: how will he then vex himself, if we tell him that the child is dead?

But when David saw that his servants whispered, David perceived that the child was dead: therefore David said unto his servants, Is the child dead? And they said, He is dead. Then David arose from the earth, and washed, and anointed himself, and changed his apparel, and came into the house of the LORD, and worshipped: then he came to his own house; and when he required, they set bread before him, and he did eat.

Then said his servants unto him, What thing is this that thou hast done? thou didst fast and weep for the child, while it was alive; but when the child was dead, thou didst rise and eat bread. And he said, While the child was yet alive, I fasted and wept: for I said, Who can tell whether GOD will be gracious to me, that the child may live? But now he is dead, wherefore should I fast? can I bring him back again? I shall go to him, but he shall not return to me. (2 Samuel 12:16-23)

David was comforted by the confidence that his little boy was "Safe in the arms of Jesus." He had gone to heaven. Furthermore, David knew that the infant would not return to earth but David would meet the child in heaven.

Some children are cared for by kind grannies, teachers and nurses but there is no care can compare with that given to the infant who has gone to be with Christ. He is a lamb In the arms of the great Shepherd and will never know any more pain, danger or evil.

Fanny Crosby, the famous American hymn writer, was an amazingly talented lady. She wrote over eight thousand hymns even though she was blind and did not begin her hymn career until she forty-four years old. These hymns have not only been instrumental in the conversion of sinners, they have also comforted many saints. Fanny was no stranger to affliction. Fanny Crosby was permanently blinded at six weeks old from a country doctor's improper medical treatment. Her father died when she was a young child and she lived her life in poverty. Later in life she lost an infant child. She felt the deep grief of empty arms and the absent child. She wrote, "I became a mother and knew a mother's love. God gave us a tender babe but the angels came and took our infant up to God and to His throne."

It was subsequent to this grief at the loss of her baby that Fanny Crosby's hymn-writing career began. Her infant child must have been on her mind when later she wrote one of the best-loved hymns of the last hundred years, "Safe in the Arms of Jesus." Of that hymn she wrote, "Dr. John Hall, in his day the famous pastor of Fifth Avenue Presbyterian Church, New York, once told me that 'Safe in the Arms of Jesus' gave more peace and satisfaction to mothers who had lost their children than any other hymn he had ever known."

In the second verse of the hymn she comforted herself by anticipating how safe and secure her little child was in God's protective care.

Safe in the arms of Jesus,
Safe from corroding care,
Safe from the world's temptations,
Sin cannot harm me there:
Free from the blight of sorrow,
Free from my doubts and fears;
Only a few more trials,
Only a few more tears.

Safe in the arms of Jesus,
Safe on His gentle breast,
There by His love o'ershaded,
Sweetly my soul shall rest.

Heaven is more real to you when you know your children are there. In the Sermon on the Mount our Saviour said, "Where your treasure is, there will your heart be also." (Matthew 6:21) Although Jesus said this in relation to our giving to God and living for God yet it also has application in reference to those children who have preceded us to heaven.

The child has been taken from the family here and that child means one of your family is in heaven. That child waits to welcome you there.

A young couple who had just lost a child spoke to Dwight L Moody about their grief and then posed the inevitable question, "Why did God let it happen?" Mr. Moody confessed that he had no easy answers to that question but he offered them comfort through an illustration. He told a story that concerned a shepherd in Europe. During the summertime when the lower valley dries up, the shepherds frequently tried to lead their sheep up a winding, thorny, and stony pathway to the higher grazing lands. The sheep, reluctant to take the difficult pathway infested with dangers and hardships, turned back and would not follow the shepherd in spite of his repeated attempts. Finally the shepherd reached into the flock and took a little lamb and placed it under his arm. He reached again and took another lamb, placing it under the other arm. He then started up the steep pathway. Soon the mother sheep started to follow the shepherd carrying the lambs. Soon afterward the entire flock followed the shepherd and climbed the tortuous trail to greener pastures.

Mr. Moody then indicated that the Great and Good Shepherd of the sheep, the Lord Jesus Christ, our Saviour, had reached into the flock and picked up their lamb. The Good Shepherd did not do it to rob the couple of their child but to lead them upward to richer and greener pastures. He wanted the parents to follow Him.

This is similar to the illustration that Rev. Workman used that night when Esther listened to him preach at the hotel., The Good Shepherd sometimes takes our little lambs so that the ewes might follow the Shepherd.

When you know the Shepherd and have faith in a living Saviour who was victorious over death and the grave, then you will someday see your little one. The apostle Paul informed the grieving Christians in Thessalonica,

But I would not have you to be ignorant, brethren, concerning them which are asleep, that ye sorrow not, even as others which have no hope...For this we say unto you by the word of the Lord, that we which are alive and remain unto the coming of the Lord shall not prevent them which are asleep. For the Lord himself shall descend from heaven with a shout, with the voice of the archangel, and with the trump of God: and the dead in Christ shall rise first: Then we which are alive and remain shall be caught up together with them in the clouds, to meet the Lord in the air: and so shall we ever be with the Lord. Wherefore comfort one another with these words. (I Thessalonians 4:13-18)

Grieving parents who understandably mourn the loss of their babies, have a right to focus on heaven   Such parents have precious treasure already over there.

God makes no mistakes. This is a hard one to accept in the midst of our grief. We all must admit that it is hard to understand why the Lord should take a little one who is dearly-loved by his parents and family and who was the centre of their lives. However, although there are undoubted mysteries in God's will we also know that God is faithful and He makes no mistakes. We can never understand the ways of God. Almost three thousand years ago Isaiah said, "For my thoughts are not your thoughts, neither are your ways my ways, saith the LORD. For as the heavens are higher than the earth, so are my ways higher than your ways, and my thoughts than your thoughts." One day we will understand.

The bereaved parent should endeavour to spend time with God. I always try to assure the bereaved parent that the little one is with the Lord and the same Lord is with us.

God comforts us so that we may comfort others. Our hurt will one day help comfort another's broken heart. Paul emphasized this when he wrote, "Blessed be God, even the Father of our Lord Jesus Christ, the Father of mercies, and the God of all comfort;   Who comforteth us in all our tribulation, that we may be able to comfort them which are in any trouble, by the comfort wherewith we ourselves are comforted of God." (2 Corinthians 1:3,4)   Grace and comfort are two words that repeatedly leap to us from 2 Corinthians. God apportions grace and comfort according to our suffering in every situation.   There then follows a chain

reaction. As God comforts us and when that comfort matures we are
then able to comfort others who in their turn will comfort others also.

Instead of focusing on yourself try to focus on the needs of others
who grieve and seek to comfort them. This can transform our grief into
hope and blessing.

Chapter eight

Wrapping Up Gravel And Making Pearls

THURSDAY MORNINGS AT DONARD SCHOOL IN BANBRIDGE, NORTHERN IRELAND, IS A SPECIAL PLACE TO BE. THESE ARE exceptional children. Thirty-six boys and girls, varying in ages from five to nineteen, most of them clad in their distinctive jade and blue uniforms, crowd into their small assembly room at the rear of the wooden-structured school. The building is tucked into the corner of the car park at the now defunct Banbridge Hospital.

Six dedicated teachers sit alongside the children as Joy Chambers strikes up the first notes on the piano of a familiar chorus. Maracas rattle, horns blast and a boy at the back row beats out the rhythm on a drum. With a surge of mingled harmony and discord the children sing,

Oh, oh, oh, How good is the Lord.
Oh, oh, oh, How good is the Lord.
Oh, oh, oh, How good is the Lord.
I never will forget what He has done for me.

He brought me salvation, How good is the Lord.
He brought me salvation, How good is the Lord.
He brought me salvation, How good is the Lord.
I never will forget what He has done for me.

The sound is terrific. These children love to sing. Their tune is not exactly on a par with the King's Chorale but they are singing from their hearts. Some bellow out the chorus so hard until the veins on their necks are clearly defined. Many of the younger children are completely off key even though Mrs. Chambers' fingers skilfully move up and down the keyboard encouraging the children's enthusiasm in song.

There is good reason to be enthusiastic on the piano. Ulster Carpets, a local manufacturing company, have just donated a brand new piano to the school and their representative is sitting at the rear of the assembled group.

Freda Wylie, the principal of the school, suggests that the children sing the chorus a little differently for the visitor from the Carpet factory. Again, in spite of the disharmony of voices, the children fervently sing:

He gave a piano. How good is the Lord.
He gave a piano. How good is the Lord.
He gave a piano. How good is the Lord.
We never will forget what He has done for us.

This chorus is followed by singing a few more favourite songs in which the boys and girls either join hands or stamp their feet. The Bible lesson takes less than ten minutes. Their attention span is limited but they are responsive to all visitors and often call out during the lesson when a response is requested and frequently at other times when it is not.

These are all special children in a special school for children with severe learning difficulties. They all have mental impairments and some have additional physical disabilities but what makes them special is not their disabilities, but the tender compassion and sacrificial care given to them Behind each of these precious lives there is a story to be told. A lot of love is showered on them by their mummies and daddies, their brothers and sisters, family friends and teachers. These are special children.

The father and mother of one child shared with me, "All our children are special to us. They are individuals with different traits and distinct characteristics. We love them equally and although there are obvious differences, we try to avoid emphasizing any difference. There are times when our Downs child needs more attention than the others but we try to share our care and attention as needed. If a child has a limitation then that child requires extra time and patience and this results in forming a special bond between the parent and the child. However, we do not treat our children differently and try to develop close relationships with them all."

❖ ❖ ❖

On a grey December day in 1989 Abbot's Cross Congregational Church was packed to capacity with an overflow crowd in the vestibule. The congregation sat in solemn and grieving silence as they listened to Rev. Tom Shaw read the Scriptures at Jeremiah 19:9: "Her sun is gone down while it was yet day:"

The preacher directed admirable and deserved words of tribute about ten-year-old Cheryl Campbell whose remains lay in the casket at the front of the church. Rev. Tom Shaw also offered a sensitive but confident message of comfort and hope to Cheryl's young parents, Philip and Catherine Campbell, who clasped each other's hand in mutual comfort as they sat listening to the minister in the front pew.

Their grief was tempered with hope and assurance. Although they had heavy hearts yet they knew that the pain and suffering were now over for their darling Cheryl. She would never again know the limitations of a physically-impaired body. Furthermore, they rested in the assurance that one day, when Jesus Christ returns, the family would be united again and together, Cheryl, with Mummy and Daddy, Paul and Joy, would go to meet the Saviour and forever be with Him.

If, as the Scriptures maintain, our lives are as a tale that is told, then behind the preaching of the minister, the empathy of family and the sympathy of friends, Philip and Catherine Campbell were closing a very important chapter in the story of their lives. Later Catherine wrote about that poignant and meaningful chapter for their family:

Panic had taken over. The pain of childbirth was so overwhelming for the young woman that she was preventing us from delivering her baby. Suddenly an older midwife stepped forward and took the young woman's face in her hands: "Listen to me," she said, "You are wasting your pain. The pain may be awful but it will produce something wonderful for you. Now don't waste your pain - use it." The situation changed immediately, for as the woman realised what her pain was all about she stopped wasting it, and I was able to deliver her beautiful baby girl a few minutes later.

How often we waste our pain, and it does not produce the wonderful results God has planned. Instead we concentrate on the anguish and the destructive forces of bitterness and anger. In the past seventeen years I have been learning to "use my pain." It has produced in me a close and deep relationship with my Saviour; a deeper understanding of the relevance of Scripture in my life; the opportunity to share with others and at times to weep with those who weep. I have come to understand what is really important in life and I am learning to value people for who they are and not for what they can do. That does not diminish the power of pain but it changes it into a constructive and positive force.

Our first baby decided to make her entrance into this world in the middle of a hot sticky summer night. To me she was the jewel in the crown of a wonderful couple of years. I had an interesting job and a lovely husband and the joy of helping him in his work of evangelism.

We were sure that soon God would open the door for us to overseas missionary service. There were no clouds to dim our sunny horizon. Then when our beautiful, blue-eyed blonde was just seven months old we were told something to turn our lives upside down.

"Mrs. Campbell, don't you realise your little girl is handicapped? She will never be normal."

The Paediatrician might as well have used a baseball bat to beat us because his words hurt just as much. So we took her home, completely unaware of how this would change our lives. This little lamb, for whom we had prayed long before she was born, had a hard road ahead, and it just did not make any sense.

Completely shattered by the news I just said: "God wouldn't do this to us, He will make it all right. It just cannot be true. We are serving the Lord. My husband is an evangelist. It just can't happen to us." But as the truth sank in I was devastated, confused, angry, and very, very hurt. Before, I had believed we were in the centre of God's will, but I couldn't believe that now.

Coming from a big church we had lots of people who called with us, assuring us of their prayers. The scripture verses they left only seemed to numb me more and I kept my pain and tears for the secrecy of my bedroom. Heartache was my constant companion and on one evening when Philip was away preaching in England I let the volcano of anguish erupt.

Then, as only God can, He came into the darkness of my situation and whispered His word to my heart. The words He used were from Isaiah 43. They had been so precious to me as a new Christian in my teens: "Fear not: for I have redeemed you, I have called you by your name; you are mine. When you pass through the waters, I will be with you; and through the rivers, they shall not overflow you: when you walk through the fire, you shall not be burned. For I am the Lord your God." In an instant I saw it. He had not promised me freedom from hard times, but that He would be right there with me through them. And for the first time I experienced what the Bible calls "the peace that passeth all understanding." God was there with me in my pain and I knew without a doubt that was where He was going to stay.

I entered a period of my life characterised by the presence and peace of God. My experience often moved from joy to disappointment, but the promise of God's presence was my constant companion. Those years were full of "firsts" and many of them heralded disappointing news of Cheryl's condition. Yet, at the same time, I was getting to know the Lord in ways I had not thought possible.

One time of immense joy was the birth of a big healthy son when Cheryl was two. Paul's arrival allowed me to enjoy the experiences of normal motherhood that had escaped me until then.

A few days before Cheryl's sixth birthday our third child was born. Having been told that our expected baby was fit and healthy, we were even more delighted when the newborn was a girl, and named her Joy. When she was put into my arms in the Labour Ward I gasped silently as she looked so like her big sister. My concern was not shared by the doctor and so I shared my worries only with my husband and God.

The days turned into weeks and to quell my nagging doubts Cheryl's Neurologist agreed to see Joy. After completing a few tests she looked tearfully at me and told me that Joy's brain had stopped growing and it was clear that she too had Microcephaly.

I remember little of the journey home except screaming at the windscreen: "That's not fair, Lord!"

I'd had six years of learning to prove God in difficult times and I just did not want any more. I had come so far spiritually but the dreadful news that Joy too would never walk, talk, or even hold her own head up, just didn't seem fair. I was so angry.

The next weeks and months were black for me, but I was to learn all over again that God really does give "Songs in the Night". In many ways God showed me that it was not a question of fairness, but a question of trust. It didn't look fair to me because I could only see things from my very limited perspective. If I could only see "the big picture" then I

would understand why I had to walk this painful way.   God showed me
that I had to trust Him with the outcome.

Not 'til the loom is silent,
And the shuttles cease to fly
Will God unfurl the canvas,
And show the reason why
The dark threads are as needful
In the Weaver's skillful hands
As the threads of gold and silver
In the pattern He has planned.

Joy's first four years were Cheryl's worst. Her health problems were
multiplying and we were told often to prepare ourselves for her death. We
started to talk to Paul of heaven and how one day soon Cheryl would get
a new body, and go to heaven to live with Jesus.

In many ways I thought I was prepared for her death, but when it
happened during the flu epidemic of 1989, the mother in me longed
to have her back. There is no doubt in my mind that grief is a cruel
experience. The fact that I had two other children didn't seem to have
much relevance to me, for I mourned for my firstborn. So much of my life
had been bound up in this little one, even my spiritual experience, that I
was plummeted to new depths of despair. Was there any reason left for
me to live? Oh, I would see my earthly years out, but would I ever really
live again?

God answered my prayer in a very direct way one Sunday afternoon in
the words of a song. As I opened my eyes after a tearful time of prayer
these words were coming through my stereo speakers:

"I've finally found the reason for living,
It's in giving every part of my heart to Him.
All that I do, every word that I say
I'll be giving it all back to Him.

For we were the reason that He gave His life
We were the reason that He suffered and died,
To a world that was lost He gave all He could give
To show us the reason to live,
He is my reason to live."

"Catherine, to be a good wife and mother is right and proper but it is not to be your reason to live. I am to be your reason to live." Just as the song had said, I was reminded of what my Saviour had done for me and it seemed to put everything back into perspective. He is indeed my reason to live, simply because of who He is. I have proved again and again that He is a Saviour worth trusting even in the dark nights of the soul.

Many years have now passed since Cheryl was born and my journey through pain began. My husband is still a busy Evangelist, my son, Paul, is a constant source of delight to us as we watch him grow into a young man who loves God. Joy is now eleven years old and although we have no idea how many more birthdays she will reach, we thank God for her sweet and uncomplaining nature that has taught us so much.

At times I wish things had been different, but then perhaps I would not have had the opportunity to experience God in the way that I have.

The lesson I learned from the old midwife all those years ago has stayed with me, for often I have felt the hands of my Saviour cup my face, and as I have looked into His eyes He has said: "Catherine, don't waste your pain. Use it, and I will make it produce wonderful things in your life."

The pain for Philip and Catherine did not end with Cheryl's death. The Campbell family continued with a strange blend of love and pain, precious memories and frustrated days, happiness which was tempered with tears. Joy lived on for another ten years during which time she suffered many similar set-backs like her sister Cheryl. She finally succumbed to death on 15th March 1999.

Again the Abbott's Cross Congregational Church was packed to capacity. Family and friends gathered in mourning to mark the passing of

another darling daughter "whose sun had gone down while it was yet
day." At that Thanksgiving Service Philip Campbell courageously gave a
moving tribute to Joy on behalf of her Mummy and Daddy:

Our Dear Joy,

Today our church is filled with people who want to
remember you and give thanks to God for the remarkable
little girl that you were. Your Mum and I felt it right to make
our own tribute to you today, for nobody knew you better
than we did.
The day you were born, our whole family rejoiced - how
could we have called you anything else but "Joy"? From that
day on, the sunshine of your smile lit up our home and our
lives. True, we were all saddened when we discovered that
- like your sister Cheryl before you - your little head showed
that you too had microcephalus. We knew then exactly the
kind of problems that lay ahead - but you just kept on smiling.
And there were lots of smiles during your short life of
thirteen and a half years probably more than people might
think.   For one thing, quite apart from the times when you
were the centre of attention, surrounded by a family who
adored you, there were many happy days in Lillian Hill's
class at Hillcroft School. When the bus came for you each
morning, we knew that both you and your friends would be
superbly looked after by the wonderful staff there. Hillcroft
was - and is - a very special place.
Of course, there was another special place you visited far
too often.   Paul Ward in the Royal Belfast Hospital for Sick
Children.   The side ward there became almost like your
second bedroom - but the nurses who cared for you there
were brilliant, weren't they? And your consultant, Dr. Elaine
Hicks always made sure you had the best of attention and

the finest possible treatment. Dr Hicks is a Paediatric Neurologist and a very clever lady, but even she was constantly baffled by how you kept on bouncing back after so many bouts of serious illness.

But I suppose we shouldn't really have been surprised - the care you received in Paul Ward was unfailingly first class. Your Mum was always there to look after you, and so many people were praying for you that God -who loves you more than we ever could - just kept answering those prayers.

It was while you were in hospital in December 1997 that it seemed your time with us was about to come to an end, but again you pulled through -surprising us all once more. You were spared to us for another fifteen months, and it does seem to us that was for a purpose.

When Tom Hill had the vision to build the first Children's Hospice here in Northern Ireland, he thought of using your story to help people realize how much it was needed and how it could help families like ours. Of course, hospices aren't needed where you are now, but maybe your contribution will help set up a service which many life-limited children and their families will be able to use and enjoy.

You know, Joy, even though you couldn't walk or talk, read or write, run and play, your life has touched lots of people - just look at how many are here today - and your Mum and I have certainly learned important lessons from you....

You showed us how to be brave in the face of suffering. We know only too well the many uncomfortable and often painful experiences you had to go through down the years. Not long ago, you were recognised by a local charity as a "Child of Courage" - but we already knew that.

You also opened many doors for us, especially into the lives of families with children who have problems like yours. Your little life became like a bridge to many hearts and many homes.

And through it all, we have learned again that "God makes no mistakes." In spite of what some might think, your life had worth and value way beyond your limitations, and our family is left much poorer because you are no longer with us.

Life without you is not going to be easy. We have loved you for more than thirteen years and we aren't going to stop now; but as we make difficult adjustments to our daily lives, how glad we are to have a super family and some wonderful friends - all of whom will be praying for us - but best of all is the Friend we have in Jesus, and we can be sure that He will never leave us nor forsake us.

The lamp beside your bed has a model of a butterfly clinging to it, and what has just happened to you has reminded us that - just as a butterfly breaks free of its chrysalis to take wings and fly, so you have been released to enjoy a whole new life with the Lord Jesus in Heaven.

In the Bible, Paul writes about how he wanted to be "Absent from the body and present with the Lord." You'll not be sorry to be 'absent' from your little body - it didn't work very well, and often it was sick and weak.

But if we could see you now - free of handicaps, chest infections and epilepsy - how could we possibly wish you back? Best of all, you're now present with the Lord, and - as Paul also said, that is "far better."

Many people have loved and cared for you down the years - apart from those we have already referred to at Hillcroft and in Paul Ward - and it would take too long to mention them all.

But we have to say that we have been blessed with a wonderful family. How could we ever have managed

without the help of your Grannies and Grandas, the love
and support of your aunties, uncles and little cousins? Paul
has always been your devoted, caring big brother, and he
will miss you just as much as we will.

Lots of people have called at our home in the past few
days, others have telephoned to say they were thinking about
us.   Did you know we have had calls from as far away as
Canada and Bolivia?   Still others have sent us cards or
letters. I know you would want us to say "thank you." to
them all.

Just yesterday a letter arrived from a Captain in the
Salvation Army, and in it he told us of a little girl he knew
who had many of the same problems you had. What he said
about her we could truthfully say about you: "She never
spoke, maybe could not see and it was doubtful whether
she could hear. Yet.. .she managed to achieve something I
have never managed in a lifetime. Her unique role was to
bring the best out of other people. Even the more
hard-bitten people would soften with her.

...she never had a bad word for any one.

...she never had an argument.

...she never (as far as I am aware) committed a sin.

...I would have been proud to have her as my daughter."

Darling Joy, we are so proud of you, and your Mum and I
thank God for the privilege of having been your parents.
Early on Monday morning, you fell asleep in your own bed,
and opened your eyes in heaven.   You must have received
quite a welcome up there - and we know you'll have one
ready for us when we see you again - and it won't be very
long till then, my Pet, it won't be long.

Philip and Catherine Campbell
17th. March 1999

❖ ❖ ❖

I feel most unworthy and in many ways unqualified to address the pain that many parents feel when their dreams for a perfect baby are not realised according to human expectations. There are no easy answers as to why children and parents are subjected to extreme suffering. I readily confess I do not understand God's purpose in the birth of a physically-handicapped or mentally-impaired child and I hope I do not traffic in unhelpful clichés in considering the problem.

Tucked away in the fine print of the genealogies of the Old Testament is the account of man who suddenly surfaces. Like one of the shooting stars of August he blazes for just a few seconds and then passes into oblivion. "And Jabez was more honourable than his brethren, and his mother called his name Jabez, saying, 'Because I bare him with sorrow (pain.)' And Jabez called on the God of Israel, saying, 'Oh that Thou wouldst bless me indeed, and enlarge my coast and that Thine hand might be with me, and that Thou wouldst keep me from evil, that it may not grieve me!' And God granted him what he requested.". (IChronicles 4:10, 11)

That is all we read about Jabez. In the middle of several chapters of tedious genealogies with difficult sounding names, God makes us stop and linger over this one man. There was something sorrowful about him as is suggested both by his name and the introduction to this man. "And" (This conjunctive word can mean "but" emphasizing the sense of contrast) his mother called his name Jabez, saying, "Because I bare him with sorrow and pain." Jabez is a descriptive title which means "pain," "distress" or even "vexation."

Why would a mother name her boy "Pain?" We are not altogether sure why it was the case, but obviously there was something vexing and anguishing about the circumstances of this baby's birth that heightened the sense of despair or hurt with his arrival. We can imagine a number of reasons why he might have gained this name:

It might have been the pain of birth.   Another story from the Old Testament indicates how the childbirth experience determined the name of a child. When Jacob's wife Rachael bore her last son she subsequently died. In her last breaths she called her son "Benoni" which means "son of my sorrow" Jacob did not comply and called his son "Benjamin" - son of my right hand.

It could have been the pain of widowhood or even single parenthood. Did the father not return from war and Jabez' mother was left a widow? For a widow or single parent to bring up a child is always difficult. It would not have been easy in those Old Testament days.

More than likely in the case of Jabez it was pain of ill-health or some handicap with the child. Whatever it was, we can conclude that Jabez got started on the wrong foot. That could have been the end of the story. However, the succinct story of Jabez demonstrates for us a man who employed his pain and handicaps to experience the blessings of God.

The story of Jabez is perhaps reflected in a principle that is mirrored in how an oyster copes with a tiny fragment of grit or sand which invades its shell. When a tiny grain of sand enters into the oyster's shell it is an unwelcome foreign body and a cruel intruder. What can the oyster do?

We are onlookers and we could think of several courses of action for the oyster. It is always easier for onlookers. The little sea creature cannot ignore the presence of pain that has befallen him. It is part of the hazard of living in the ocean. Pain is a reality and it happens in the oyster's world. In our fallen planet we are subject to many perils also.

The oyster might be justified in rebelling or complaining against the circumstances that brought the unwelcome grit into its life.   That is the course of action that many men and women adopt in times of adversity and trouble and they pose the question "Why should this have to happen to me? What have I done to deserve this?"

However, the oyster does not take that course of action. Complaining and rebelling do not do the oyster any good, for when all the protests and complaints are finished, the grain of sand would still be there.

Another attitude the oyster could adopt calls for a lot of fortitude and
courage and determination. The oyster could say, "This hard calamity
has overtaken me and I can't reverse it. It hurts and I wish it wasn't here.
I will just have to endure it for the rest of my life." Life is hard enough
without having to put up with our lot. We must learn not to waste our
pain. Time is too short for that.

None of these attitudes are adopted by the oyster. He recognizes the
presence of the harsh intruder. It is not alone in its hardship for this
same thing happens to many oysters. It is part of the risk of living in the
sea world. However, right away the oyster begins to do something about
it.

Slowly and patiently the oyster works with the grain of sand. He
wraps layer upon layer of a creamy, milky substance around each sharp
corner and coats over every cutting edge. Gradually and ever so slowly
the oyster keeps on wrapping up his troubles until a beautiful pearl is
eventually made. A pearl is just the oyster's trouble wrapped around with
a thing of wondrous beauty. The oyster has learned to turn grains of sand
into pearls, the initial pain of grit and distress into wondrous grace.

No wonder the Bible speaks of pearly gates. They are testimony to
the grace of our Lord Jesus Christ. The pain, suffering, death and blood-
shedding that our Saviour bore bought us an open way to heaven. But
God can also help us to make pearls from the painful intruders in our
lives.

Some truths to help us wrap up our troubles in such difficult times are
found in the Scriptures.

God loves our children – and He loves us too. Our Saviour
demonstrated His love for children so many times. They are all precious
to Him. He took children on His knee. He prayed for them and blessed
them. Whatever handicap a child might have does not invalidate or
devalue God's estimation of that child. If we humans, as parents, family,
friends and teachers can show love and compassion to those children
with multiple impairments how much more does our heavenly Father care

for them. The Lord Jesus spoke of children when He said, "Take heed that ye despise not one of these little ones; for I say unto you, That in heaven their angels do always behold the face of my Father which is in heaven." (Matthew 18:10) Children are precious to Him.

God has secured their destiny. Christian parents shall see their handicapped sons and daughters in heaven. The handicaps will be gone. Such children who are incapable of comprehending spiritual matters and making spiritual choices are provided for by the grace of God in the atonement made by Jesus Christ. The Lord said, "And they shall be mine, saith the LORD of hosts, in that day when I make up my jewels;" (Malachi 3:17) We often sing Pastor William Cushing's hymn which he wrote for the children of his own Sunday School in 1856:

When He cometh, when he cometh
To make up His jewels,
All His jewels, precious jewels,
His loved and His own.

Like the stars of the morning,
His bright crown adorning,
They shall shine in their beauty-
Bright gems for His crown.

He will gather, He will gather
The gems for His kingdom,
All the pure ones, all the bright ones,
His loved and His own.

Little children, little children
Who love their Redeemer,
Are the jewels, precious jewels,
His loved and His own.

The scriptural promise of Christ's Second Coming is thrilling truth for believers to ponder and a prospect that brings comfort to our grieving hearts. For that reason it is important that parents come to know the Saviour also.

Peter, a pupil at Donard School, has good reading and comprehension skills. One day he approached Mrs. Wylie and posed the question, "Do you know somewhere in John that speaks of Jesus as the only begotten Son of God or is it the only forgotten Son of God?" Unwittingly he touched on an aspect of our attitude to Jesus Christ that people do well to consider. Freda Wylie confesses that there is never a day when she leaves the school without having learnt something from her pupils.

God is in control of every life. As Christians we maintain that God is Sovereign and is in control of everything in our lives. That is fundamental and basic. He not only created all things but He made us the people we are.

"For thou hast possessed my reins: thou hast covered me in my mother's womb. I will praise thee; for I am fearfully and wonderfully made: My substance was not hid from thee, when I was made in secret, and curiously wrought in the lowest parts of the earth. Thine eyes did see my substance, yet being unperfect; and in thy book all my members were written, which in continuance were fashioned, when as yet there was none of them." (Psalm 139:13-16)

I remember sharing in a conference when under discussion was Paul's challenge to the Roman Christians, "I beseech you therefore brethren that ye present your bodies..." One pastor pointed out that we often take for granted this is speaking of an able and healthy body. He drew attention to the fact that one of his sons had a physical handicap. The pastor maintained that the Lord gave his son this body and therefore that is the body they offered back to God.

As Christians we believe God is in control of what we go through in life. As Catherine Campbell expressed, "Everything that comes to us is

Father-filtered." However, we have the responsibility of how we go through it. I agree with the statement made by Chuck Swindoll, "Life is ten percent stuff, and ninety percent of how we respond to that stuff." As Catherine Campbell expressed, we should not waste our pain. Like the oyster we need to employ it for the good of others and the glory of God.

Disabilities and handicaps have a purpose. As I have already admitted, I do not understand why one family can be gifted with a seemingly perfect infant while another child is born with physical and mental impairments. Our understanding is limited. Our Saviour on one occasion was asked about a man who was born blind: "And his disciples asked him, saying, Master, who did sin, this man, or his parents, that he was born blind? Jesus answered, Neither hath this man sinned, nor his parents: but that the works of God should be made manifest in him." (John 9:2,3)

The Lord Jesus healed that blind man and used his testimony to demonstrate the grace of God. The Lord still uses all means that are wrapped in the mystery of His providence to accomplish His purpose.

The parents from Donard Special School with whom I spoke indicated that for the first seven years they found it difficult to come to terms with their child's so-called imperfections. It was only when they recognised that God had sent their son into their home that they were able to recognise also God had a purpose in doing so. It was then that they handed their child back to God and were able to accept their boy's Downs syndrome.

Physically and mentally impaired children constrain parents, family and friends to sacrificial love and service. Many parents of children with physical or mental deficiencies do not look on their love for their children as sacrifice. They love their children because they are their children, born into their family. However, if a cup of cold water given in the Name of the Lord shall not lose its reward and the Saviour specifically promised that whatever was done for one of these little ones it was done unto Him, how much more does the Lord consider those who care for children who are totally dependent on the parents.

It is in coping with such needy children that parents and friends sacrifice time pour out love and intercede in prayer for little ones who cannot pray for themselves. Such love and sacrifice do not go unrewarded. In spite of what physical or mental impairment children may have they have a way of reciprocating their love without speaking a word.

Physically and mentally impaired children help us concentrate on priorities. While many around us are caught up in accomplishment and trying to be successful these little ones struggle with survival. They teach us how frail we are and how transient our life is.

In many ways they have it right. Some may look on them and call them "handicapped." Why should we classify them as handicapped while we excuse the terrorist, the rapist and the child molester? Each of these children has a distinct personality. I have found that they have two great priorities; to enjoy security of being loved and have the opportunity of expressing their love. I suggest we are all handicapped who do not have these priorities.

Freda Wylie, Principal of the Donard Special School in Banbridge, penned the following poem after a bomb was planted in Banbridge and the terrible atrocity in which twenty-nine people died as a result of a bomb in Omagh in August 1998. She declared, "I wrote this poem looking at things from the eyes of one of my very special people."

People are strange you know
They like labels
Nice neat categories, especially in our land
Prod, Mick, Black, White, Orange, Green
Nice neat boxes

More labels, clever, thick and worse
Softly spoken "not right you know"
Or as I was marked, politically correct
Special needs, learning difficulties
Or even a strange sounding syndrome.

Yes, I know I am slower than some
I take some time to do the simple tasks,
Things that you, my so-called right-minded friend
Call easy, take for granted.

My pleasures are innocent
I liked T.V.
Until tonight, while waiting for my programmes
I saw the news, the scenes of hurt in Omagh
The prams, the pain, the wheelchair and the blood.

My life is filled with love
My family friends and school
I hear strange sounds
Protestant, Catholic, what mean these words?
I see only caring in the eyes of those I meet.

Why then, these pictures on my screen?
Babies, mums and dads.
There is something really wrong
I'm not sure what.

I heard them say, whisper even,
When I was small,
Different, this child has special needs
But how? I love, receive love in return

With simple mind I know
That I am right and they are very wrong
The evil men
Who bomb and kill and maim

Yes I am right and they are wrong
Dear God, change hearts that choose to warp in hate
Those with minds and limbs intact,
It's them with special needs, needing help
Without the dispensation I possess
If being different, not by choice
But accident of birth.

Physically and mentally impaired children have a full life. We tend to measure life by quantity of years and quality of health. Some of the choicest saints have suffered great hardships and pains. The race of life can be a short one but a full one. It was short for Cheryl and Joy Campbell but they made a full impact on many others. Such lives humble us, they make us thankful for what we have received and most certainly help us to see God's grace in Philip's and Catherine's family.

Said Catherine Campbell,

It's as if we went from one hurdle to the next, but I'm glad that I had the Lord to help me over those hurdles. I had my weepy days, I still do, but that shows I am human. Some say there is no hope, but Cheryl had a purpose and a quality in her life that God gave her. We saw God's plans being worked out even in her wee life.

Philip Campbell added,

Some people don't like to think about death and heaven, but God has shown me there is so much to look forward to. Cheryl's and Joy's lives were not worthless. They had been very precious to us and I wouldn't have changed the real them. We are sustained knowing that our two girls are with Christ which is far better. Down here they could not walk, but now they are walking the streets of glory. Down here they could not see, but now they are looking upon the face of Jesus. Down here they could not talk but now they are singing the praises of Christ. We could not keep going without God, he is our refuge and strength, a very present help in times of trouble. God has his purpose in all these things even though we may not see it now.

Cheryl and Joy Campbell were God's gifts to Philip and Catherine Campbell. He entrusted these two darling daughters to a couple who would care for them and pour tons of love upon them. For over twenty years and through all their heartaches and trials, Philip and Catherine confirmed that God's grace is greater than all human difficulties and His strength is sufficient for all our weakness.

Cheryl and Joy have gone to heaven but their influence lives on in Philip's and Catherine's pastoral ministry at Coleraine Congregational Church. Catherine Campbell has an additional ministry to parents who are still trying to come to terms with handling the sort of difficulties they experienced. Furthermore, as Philip pointed out, Cheryl and Joy do not need a hospice any more. However, their lives helped inspire others in the setting up Northern Ireland's first Children's Hospice for the benefit of other children.

These are only a few of the benefits that have flowed from their legacy and memory. We can only see a little part of the bigger picture at present. One day we will fully understand.

Chapter nine

Homosexuality Reverses God's Order

I WAS NONCHALANTLY LISTENING TO A MAGAZINE PROGRAMME ON BBC RADIO FOUR AS I DROVE THROUGH NARROW WINDING roads of lowland Scotland. The beautiful heather-clad hills rose steeply on either side of the tarmac and although keeping my mind on the road, I was enjoying the serenity of the tranquil countryside en route to my destination. Suddenly I was jolted out of my casual listening to the radio when one of several journalists spoke up about some of the funniest things children say. He said on the programme that he had a most embarrassing experience when his five-year-old girl came running into the kitchen of their home and asked, "Daddy, what is a lesbian?"

The embarrassed father immediately looked around for his wife to come to the rescue but she was not at home. She had gone to the shops. He confessed that he was faced with a dilemma – what should he say to his daughter who was waiting for a reply and was confident her dad knew everything. In a flash his mind wrestled with three questions, "Do I ignore her? Do I tell her a lie? Do I tell her the truth?" He recognised to tell a lie or ignore the child would be wrong so he opted to tell his daughter what a lesbian was.

Calmly he sat the girl down and in simple non-embarrassing terms he tried to explain to the pre-schooler what a lesbian was. When he had finished the young daughter seemed completely satisfied with Dad's answer and returned to play with her friends outdoors.

Just after the episode the child's mother arrived home laden with her purchases. The husband was glad to see her and the first thing with which he greeted her was the incident that had just happened. He explained to his wife how the daughter wanted to know what a lesbian was.

"You didn't tell her?" the surprised mother snapped with a frown on her face.

"I did. I was as diplomatic as I could be and told her the truth in simple language."

"You fool!" said his incensed wife. "It was not lesbians she is asking about. It is the new neigbours next door. She has been asking about them for days. They are Wesleyans but she cannot pronounce the word."

I smiled at the anecdote but there is nothing funny about homosexuality. It is not funny for the victims or the families affected by those who adopt this lifestyle.

I find it alarming how much our society has become exposed and acclimatised to homosexuality. For sometime both in the United States and in United Kingdom, the population has been experiencing a sexual revolution. Several decades ago homosexual relationships and other unnatural sexual activities were not only deemed illegal, they carried with them a sense of shame. Now they have not only become socially acceptable to many but some of those who indulge in such practices flaunt this unseemly lifestyle on society as a whole. In the United Kingdom we have long since left behind the debate about the legitimacy of homosexuality. Now the conflict centres on the minimum age for consenting adults involved in this activity.

Homosexuals are readily found in responsible positions in industry, banking, professional life and even in government not to mention their high profile and celebrity status in the entertainment world. Not only do leading politicians openly admit their same sex relationships, but frequently the general public, knowing the lifestyle of the political candidate, return him or her for public office. As I heard one preacher say recently. "We used to hide these people in the closet. Now we have them in the cabinet." As for the entertainment world it seems that there is mileage to be gained for openly admitting an alternative sexual preference.

Just recently a case hit the headlines in United Kingdom of two homosexual males who had been in a live-in relationship for a considerable time. They employed the services of a surrogate mother in United States who underwent artificial insemination by the sperm of one of the men and bore twin girls for the homosexual couple. The two men have since brought the twins back to England. The limits to which the gay lobbyists will push their lifestyle seem to have no bounds.

However, homosexuality in its various forms is not limited to the secular world outside Christendom. For quite some time the Church of England has been rent with schism over the matter of so called "gay clergy and gay Christians." In Ireland there are almost weekly revelations of homosexual practices which were practiced for decades under the cloak of secrecy in religious institutions.

The November 1999 edition of "The Evangelical Times", United Kingdom's leading monthly evangelical newspaper, carried a short and sad report about one of England's leading preachers,

"News that Roy Clements, pastor of Eden Chapel Cambridge, had left his wife and family and was involved in a relationship with another man has shocked Evangelicals everywhere. Mr. Clements was an influential preacher and apologist for evangelical doctrine. He travelled widely, speaking at conferences, and was a senior figure in the Evangelical Alliance as well as a regular contributor to a number of evangelical periodicals. He is the author of several books.

Mr. Clements resigned from the church pastorate several months ago, after twenty-five years in the ministry. It was following this period of leave that he told his wife of twenty-nine years that he was ending their marriage. Mr. Clements, who has three children, has moved out of the family home. Church elders tried unsuccessfully to dissuade him from his course of action.

The identity of the other man has not been revealed, but it is thought he may have been a church member. In a press statement, the Evangelical Alliance described the relationship as 'celibate,' though it is unclear what is meant by this term. What is clear is that Mr. Clements has committed serious sin by breaking up his marriage to pursue a lifestyle condemned by Scripture.

The news of the marriage break-up made the national press and brings the cause of Christ into disrepute."

In Philip Yancey's great book, "What's So Amazing About Grace?" he relates the story of a close friend who had worked alongside some of foremost conservative evangelicals in the United States. For several decades he concealed from them that he was homosexual. When he disclosed that he had a homosexual orientation he shocked the evangelical world.

Christians are sometimes looked on as being homophobic but there can be no more earth-shattering news for a partner or a parent than to hear his wife, her husband, son or daughter announce, "I'm a homosexual." The discovery of homosexuality in a family member may be communicated by a letter received, a frank admission from the party concerned or sometimes the accidental stumbling on the evidence of the practice. Whatever way it comes there is no easy way to handle it. How would you cope if the following letter was addressed to you?

Dear Mum and Dad,

Thank you for your love and for our home. I cannot tell you this to your face for I know it would only hurt you too much. I know you had great plans for me and looked forward to a nice wedding. Mum we live in different times. I have met

Jane and we are setting up home together. I find I have
more in common with her than with a man. I love Jane. I
hope you can understand.

I love you,

Whack! Wham! Bang! It would be a horrendous experience for any
right-thinking parents to receive such a letter. It is enough to drive them
to the brink of insanity and for many it does.

Barbara Johnson, one of America's best-loved Christian authors,
recounts in many of her books the shock and horror she and her husband
suffered when they accidentally discovered that their Christian son Larry,
was a practicing homosexual.   Bill and Barbara Johnson had already lost
two sons. One was killed in the Vietnam War less than six months after
being drafted. The other son and his friend were killed in a traffic
accident in Alaska. These two tragedies broke their hearts.

Bill and Barbara still have two other sons – Larry and Barny. Barny
was very much a home bird but Larry travelled in Christian service. He
had not only been raised in a Christian home but was engaged in a
Christian musical ministry which took him all over the United States.
When Bill and Barbara stumbled on their son's secret lifestyle they were
crushed and dumbfounded. Like many other parents who have made this
discovery they swung from one emotion to another; numbed, devastated,
angry, ashamed, guilty, with floods of tears through it all.

When they verified that their discovery was true they were sure they
could "fix it" when they pointed out to their son how wrong it was. They
were certain he would soon change his way. They were wrong. It did not
work that way. The confrontation between the parents and their
son introduced a rift in the family which took years to heal. Through
persistent praying in which Bill and Barbara did not give up, there were
floods of tears, years of patience and buckets of unconditional love until
they finally saw their son restored to Jesus Christ and the family.

WHAT IS HOMOSEXUALITY?

The Oxford dictionary defines a homosexual as "person sexually attracted only by persons of one's own sex." A homosexual woman is known as a Lesbian, a word derived from the Greek Island of Lesbos in the Aegean which was home of Sapphos.

We should be aware that not all homosexuals are necessarily effeminate men or masculine women or are they limited to any one class of society. Sometime during the last thirty years homosexuality gained the euphemism "gay" which previously had been quite an innocuous word.

Much laboratory research has been done by non-Christian scientists to prove that homosexuality is genetic. Much to the surprise of the scientists they had to conclude that homosexuality is environmentally induced. As Christians we believe that God who condemns homosexuality, as the Creator of all things He did not create a homosexual gene.

Dr. Charles Swindoll maintains that strictly speaking there is no such thing as a homosexual. There is a difference between being homosexual and acting homosexually and denying the crucial elements of one's own gender.

The circumstances and environment that induces homosexuality may reach far back into a person's past. However, at some point a definite decision is made to indulge in homosexual behaviour. Likewise the homosexual, aided by God and the power of the gospel, can make a decision to cease from this conduct.

HOMOSEXUALITY AND THE BIBLE.

The Bible speaks with a clear, direct voice against homosexuality. Both God's plans for marriage and His repudiation of homosexuality give a strong message that same sex relationship is not God's design for his creatures. Genesis 2:18-25 provides us with God's perfect plan for marriage. The Lord said, "It is not good that the man should be alone; I will make him an help meet for him." Until the creation of Eve, Adam was alone. There was no one who was suitable for him as a companion to love. God made him a suitable help meet – a female who "answered back" to Adam's masculinity.

God's provision for Adam was Eve as the one whom he could and did love in a heterosexual relationship as God had planned. This first marriage of male and female is a standard that is consistently upheld throughout the rest of the Bible both in Old Testament and New Testament.

The Bible frequently addresses the matter of homosexuality, which in the Scriptures is called "sodomy," and always treats it as sin, unnatural and an abomination unto the Lord The practice gained the name "sodomy" in the Bible because of the first record of such a practice.

In Genesis 19:1-13 the story of Lot and his family in Sodom and Gomorrah shows God's antipathy toward the godless culture where men desired relationships with men rather than the daughters of Lot. After Lot and the family were dragged out of the immoral quagmire, God visited His judgment on the twin cities of the plain.

In Leviticus God gave details on how His people were to follow a different pattern from the surrounding cultures. "Thou shalt not lie with mankind, as with womankind: it is abomination." (Lev. 18:22) "If a man also lie with mankind, as he lieth with a woman, both of them have committed an abomination: they shall surely be put to death; their blood shall be upon them." (Lev. 20:13)

JUDGES 19:10-30

The sad story in Judges 19:10-30 tells of a traveller who arrived in the city of Gibeah and gave his defenseless concubine to a mob of men who waited outside their dwelling. Poor girl! The men "took his concubine, and brought her forth unto them; and they knew her, and abused her all the night until the morning: and when the day began to spring, they let her go." (v25) However, sadder still is that the concubine was not their real object of the depraved desires and lust of these sons of Belial. They really wanted the man. Judges 19:22 informs us that they "beset the house round about, beat at the door, and spake to the master of the house, the old man, saying, Bring forth the man that came into thine house, that we may know him." God judged them for their debased and perverted lust.

Perhaps Romans 1:26-27 gives us the most sweeping view of God's estimate of homosexuality. Almost like the descending side of a moral escalator the Apostle Paul gives a step by step catalogue of the spiritual and moral downfall of all men as God gave the human race up to their base corruption. One downward stride in the descent was when men and women exchanged heterosexuality for homosexuality and burned " in their lust one toward another.

"And changed the glory of the uncorruptible God into an image made like to corruptible man, and to birds, and fourfooted beasts, and creeping things. Wherefore God also gave them up to uncleanness through the lusts of their own hearts, to dishonour their own bodies between themselves: Who changed the truth of God into a lie, and worshipped and served the creature more than the Creator, who is blessed for ever. Amen. For this cause God gave them up unto vile affections: for even their women did change the natural use into that which is against nature: And likewise also the men, leaving the natural use of the woman, burned in their lust one toward another; men with men working that which is unseemly, and receiving in themselves that recompence of their error which was meet." Romans 1:23 27

Charles Swindoll in his Counselling Manual points out that Paul displays this step in man's sinful descent not because homosexuality is universal but because it shows that man's bent toward sin is universal. Humankind is so intent on sinning that we will cross even the boundaries of nature to do so."

We conclude that the Scriptures are clear in teaching that homosexuality is an abomination unto God and a mark of extreme degeneration that characterised the pagan nations. It is therefore difficult to see how any one can justify homosexuality and yet believe the Bible to be God's Word.

However, the Bible has more to say about homosexuals and others who indulge in such perverted abuses. Corinth was a pagan city but many Corinthians came to know the Lord Jesus Christ as Saviour. Some of those converts had been abusers of themselves with mankind.

"Know ye not that the unrighteous shall not inherit the kingdom of God? Be not deceived: neither fornicators, nor idolaters, nor adulterers, nor effeminate, nor abusers of themselves with mankind, Nor thieves, nor covetous, nor drunkards, nor revilers, nor extortioners, shall inherit the kingdom of God. And such were some of you: but ye are washed, but ye are sanctified, but ye are justified in the name of the Lord Jesus, and by the Spirit of our God." (I Corinthians 6:9-11)

William Barclay, in his "The Letters to the Corinthians," wrote, "Homosexuality swept like a cancer through Greece and from Greece invaded Rome. We can scarcely realize how riddled the ancient world was with it. Even so great a man as Socrates practiced it; Plato's dialogue The Symposium is said to be one of the greatest works on love in the world, but its subject is unnatural love. Fourteen out of the first fifteen Roman emperors practiced this unnatural vice. During this time Nero was emperor. He had taken a boy called Sporus and had him castrated. He then married him with a full marriage ceremony and took him home in procession to his palace and lived with him.... When Nero was eliminated and Otho came to the throne, one of the first things he did was take possession of Sporus. Much later than this the Emperor Hadrian's name is forever associated with a Bithynian youth called Antinous. He lived with him inseparably, and when he died he deified him and covered the world with statues that immortalized his sin by calling a star after him." This report indicates that homosexuality was a prevailing practice among the Roman authorities and widespread among the general population.

However, there is good news for those who have been enslaved to this unnatural and perverted habit. The Bible reminds us that a fountain has been opened for all sin and uncleanness. "The blood of Jesus Christ His Son cleanseth us from all sin." These Corinthians were washed clean from their sins and set apart for better use. No matter what your past may be there is forgiveness and cleansing for all in the blood of Jesus Christ.

WHY BOTHER? WHAT HARM DOES IT DO?

There is abroad an increasing aggressive militancy about the right of homosexuals to choose their own lifestyle. Often we hear people say, "We should not oppose the lifestyle of others if that is what they want to do." To say this is to close our eyes to the implications of unnatural sexual activities on the whole society. Would we use the same yardstick and be as tolerant on a person who adopts a lifestyle of rape, incest or sexual abuse of children?

Like other violations of God's laws, homosexuality is a dangerous practice. Everyone agrees that if you drive down the wrong side of the road you can expect to be injured or even killed. Homosexual practices take us down the wrong side of the road. It will expose the victim to much physical and psychological danger and will put society in jeopardy.

I have found that homosexuals fall into these categories:

Denial: Even though many homosexuals carry out their unnatural lifestyle quite openly and are quick to form "gay rights" organisations, there are still many who live a double life and indulge in homosexual activities under a cloak of secrecy. They will deny outright any such inclination or involvement and often conceal their habit either because of guilt or the fear of the consequences of being discovered.

Deceit: Frequently the homosexual's covertness and secrecy about their unnatural ways forces him or her to be deceptive in the front they portray to others. This is especially true in the Christian fraternity where exposure of homosexuality invites censure and discipline.

Demanding: Those who candidly admit their homosexual practices often strive for acceptability of their lifestyle and even encourage others to engage in it.

I find it difficult in the light of these Scriptures to accept the views of those in the evangelical world who can accommodate the homosexual lifestyle as a natural orientation on a par with single parent families and accepted on the same basis. We do not necessarily approve of the single parent family but one wrong does not allow for another and especially when it has such a detrimental effect on society.

IS THERE HOPE FOR THE HOMOSEXUAL?

Yes there is hope. The Devil would have the guilt-ridden homosexual feel there is no hope and no way out of the mesh in which they have become entangled. God assures all sinners there is hope for change and forgiveness. As Christians we need to be careful not to adopt such a moralist attitude which in effect becomes a barrier to that person finding hope in Jesus Christ.

We should recognise that in the sight of God the practicing homosexual is no worse and no better than the immoral heterosexual. All immorality is a threat to society and if left unrestrained it will bring disastrous consequences on the population. However, just as there is no distinction between white lies and black lies, so also there are no "special sins" before God. All men and women are declared to be sinners against God who has provided salvation for all sin in Jesus Christ. God calls all men to repent from their sins and receive Jesus Christ as Saviour.

The real solution to the problem of homosexuality and all immorality is a personal relationship with Jesus Christ. He will make the repentant sinner a new creation. The best way to sever a homosexual relationship is to have a new relationship to God. Just as those Corinthian Christians previously had indulged in immoral lifestyles, by receiving Jesus Christ their lives were transformed by the power of the gospel of Jesus Christ.

The dynamic of the gospel is not to destroy lives but to put them together again. Jesus Christ said that he was sent to heal the brokenhearted, preach deliverance to the captives and liberty to the oppressed. (See Luke 4:18,19)

I do recognise that to break away from this adopted life style may be difficult and painful. However, with God on his side the forgiven sinner can be an overcomer. God has made provision for us: "If we confess our sins he is faithful and just to forgive us our sins and to cleanse us from all unrighteousness." (I John 1:9)

God will not only forgive our sin but He has promised to support us in the time of temptation, "There hath no temptation taken you but such as is common to man: but God is faithful, who will not suffer you to be tempted above that ye are able; but will with the temptation also make a way to escape, that ye may be able to bear it."

HELPING THE HOMOSEXUAL.

Attitude: For a church there is the responsibility of exercising discipline which encourages repentance for the Christian who has fallen into sexual perversions. The thrust of Paul's command to the Corinthians to "deliver such a one to Satan for the destruction of the flesh" is to the unrepentant offender. The person concerned in the Corinthian Church not only continued in his sin but the church bragged about it and took no action. (See I Corinthians 5)

The motive behind excommunication from the church, which Paul commanded, was to encourage the person to repent and be restored. It was probably to the same man, now repentant of his immoral sin, that Paul referred in 2 Corinthians 2:5-8;

But if any have caused grief, he hath not grieved me, but in part: that I may not overcharge you all. Sufficient to such a man is this punishment, which was inflicted of many. So that contrariwise ye ought rather to forgive him, and comfort him, lest perhaps such a one should be swallowed up with overmuch sorrow. Wherefore I beseech you that ye would confirm your love toward him.

Paul explained that it was time to forgive the man who had been punished by the church. Obviously he had subsequently repented from his sins. The church was to comfort, restore and accept him. Prolonged and unjustified exclusion from the church would give Satan advantage over the man.

The church should be like a hospital, caring for the wounded in whatever state we find them. We endeavour to help those who are caught up in the drug scene or alcoholism, but somehow we shy away from helping to restore homosexuals and exclude them from the church. There is a time for discipline and a time to restore the disciplined person.

However, we have got to recognize that there are Christians who are struggling with this addiction, and addiction it is, but they are fearful of disclosing their lifestyle to anyone as they know they will be shunned. Sadly, as young people growing up many were introduced to this practice through older men and frequently were unaware of its nature and consequences. Addiction sets in and they are ensnared even though they hate this lifestyle and struggle against the overpowering temptation.

Even when repentant homosexuals come to faith in Christ, they still find it difficult to be completely free from this snare and they long to be able to ask for help, but alas they are so often condemned if they broach the subject. There are very few Christians who are unafraid to reach out in love and support them until they are completely free from this addiction.

Individually, it is hard to be objective when confronted with homosexuality, especially if that person is a friend or family member. We should ask God for grace and wisdom in the situation. It is possible to be frank about their abhorrent practice and yet assure the person that you care for them. Our Saviour was always frank but always compassionate. While we may take a strong stand alongside the Scriptures it is important that we use the Word of God as a Sword to pierce with conviction and as not a club to batter the homosexual. We must make clear that although God hates homosexuality He does not hate the homosexual.

Prayer: While you stand by the truth of the Scripture in relation to the homosexual yet commit the person to God in prayer.   Prayer changes things - and people too. Be prepared to persevere with prayer in spite of disregard for your admonition for them to change.

Counselling: There may be behavioural and environmental elements that have contributed to the victim's lifestyle. Encourage the person to seek help and assure them that there is forgiveness when they confess their homosexual practice as sin and are prepared to forsake it. While Christians justly abhor the homosexual lifestyle they should always be the first to help where there is an admission of guilt.

All our dealings with people who are caught in a web of homosexuality should be modelled on how the Lord Jesus related to sinners. Remember, but for the grace of God it could be us.

Chapter ten

Suicide Answers Nothing

IT WAS ANOTHER BRIGHT BRAZILIAN MORNING. THE HOT SUN WAS RISING IN THE SKY ABOVE THE REMOTE TOWN OF TARAUACA located on a tributary over two and a half thousand miles from the mouth of the River Amazon. The town had been a hive of activity from when the sun first appeared at 5:30 a.m. The town's folk were busy going about their daily business - oxen pulled carts laden with raw rubber latex and children clad in their navy and white school uniforms made their way to school.

Dr. Tom Geddis was the local missionary doctor, but he and his wife Ethel had left Tarauaca for a prolonged furlough in United Kingdom. Their absence left the town without any qualified medical practitioner. Periodically doctors were financed by various politicians to visit the town for a few days.

I also was a missionary in Tarauaca, but a year at the Missionary School of Medicine in London and working alongside Dr. Tom at the hospital allowed me to keep the small hospital functioning. Besides some elementary dental work which mostly involved extractions under local anaesthetic, I treated the sick as best I could. Often I was called to cases that frightened the life out of me. I am aware that a little knowledge is a dangerous thing but when faced with situations of either life or death then I had to be prepared for many contingencies. These included treating snake bites, suturing wounds, administering blood transfusions and sometimes even helping in the delivery of difficult births.

Besides these emergencies I was frequently called on by the mayor and the local chief of police to be the town coroner. This entailed signing all death certificates and giving police reports on any violent deaths which happened, and this was an all too common occurrence.

It was in the course of discharging this latter responsibility that I met Jose. He and his family had lived in a simple dwelling on the outskirts of our small town which was completely surrounded on three sides by lush green forest and bordered on the fourth side by a tributary of the great Amazon River. Jose, like many in the region, had become embroiled in a vendetta of vengeance.

He had killed a man who previously had murdered a member of Jose's family in retaliation for an earlier killing. These chains of reprisals and revenge often go back generations. As a result of being arrested, charged and found guilty of murder he was sentenced to life in prison. However, Tarauaca did not have a secure penitentiary for such criminals so for over two years Jose lived under a sort of house-arrest.

While I was at the hospital one morning I heard the familiar drone of an approaching aircraft. It was an old Dakota plane of the Brazilian Airforce. The aircraft was transporting several police officers from Rio Branco the capital of Acre, to apprehend prisoners such as Jose and take them to the State Penitentiary. At Tarauaca some officers disembarked to round up the local criminals while the plane left for the neighbouring town of Cruzeiro do Sul, one hour's flight away. The aircraft would return four hours later to transport prisoners and officers to the capital.

When Jose heard that he was to be suddenly snatched away from his house-arrest and from his family to be incarcerated far from home he determined he would never go.

Just after lunch several local police officers arrived at the front door of our wooden house and said that the chief of police needed to see me. I mounted my Honda 90 motor cycle and in the hot sun of the midday I sped through the dusty streets to the Police Station. From there I travelled with several police officers in a rickety old jeep towards the outskirts of town and finally arrived at Jose's house.

The family was in deep shock. Piercing wails emanated from inside the wooden house. I found Jose's body fifty yards from the house. The shotgun lay at his side where he fell. The thought of penitentiary was too much for him. He could not cope with the anticipation of being isolated from his family. In a moment of insanity he violently and prematurely brought down the curtains on his short life.

❖ ❖ ❖

Judy was a fine-looking young lady in her mid-twenties. She attended meetings I conducted in 1978 in a township just outside Philadelphia in United States of America. She was a teacher in grade school and seemed to be full of life and vigour. After one of our Sunday morning meetings Judy waited behind and trusted Jesus Christ as her personal Saviour.

Following her conversion she had great swings between doubt and assurance of her salvation. Her past life and involvement in drugs haunted her. Those close to her tried to encourage Judy but know one knew just how deep her problem was. It was a terrible shock to her family and acquaintances when Judy was found hanging at the end of a rope on a Saturday morning.

❖ ❖ ❖

Early in 1999 "Screaming Lord Sutch," the man who brought a dash of colour and a smile to British politics, hanged himself after losing a twenty-year battle against depression. In a note found beside his body by his fiancée, the leader of the Official Monster Raving Loony Party wrote: "I can't cope any longer."

Yvonne Elwood revealed that despite his public image as a lighthearted eccentric, Sutch was tormented in his private life. "He may have seemed to be a very happy man but it was all just a front. He suffered from depression for twenty years and just couldn't take it any more. Over the past few years he'd been taking Prozac. It masked the symptoms, but I suppose he became immune to its effects after a while."

According to close friends, Sutch grew more depressed after the death of his beloved Yorkshire terrier Rosie a few weeks before his death. Former Rolling Stones drummer Carlo Little, who had known Sutch since the Sixties, said, "His little dog died a few days ago and David took it very badly. She was the last link with his mother; who passed away two years ago and whom he adored. The death of the two of them hit him hard."

The body of 58-year-old Sutch was discovered by his girlfriend Yvonne. The pair were due to marry in Las Vegas in October 1999 and were in daily contact by phone. Yvonne wept as she said: "We were so happy together and had so much to look forward to." She admitted that Sutch had talked about suicide before, but she refused to be drawn on whether he had ever tried to take his own life.

❖ ❖ ❖

During almost forty years of Christian ministry both as a pastor and missionary, I have had the grievous experience of helping families pick up the pieces after a tragic suicide in the family. Some have been the simplest people in the jungles of Brazil who had laden their bodies with heavy weights and then slipped into the muddy waters of the river in the middle of the night. Others have been part of our modern and sophisticated society who ended their lives from a deliberate overdose of tablets or the blast of a gun. These cases have involved young people as well as older, men as well as women.

In 1978 Jim Jones led nine hundred and twelve members of his cult to mass suicide in Jonestown, Guyana, which was not too far over the border from where we lived in the Amazon. More recently thirty-nine members of the Heaven's Gate cult committed group suicide in 1997 in the belief that a space-ship was behind the approaching Hale-Bopp comet and it would convey them to their salvation after they left this life.

The present day emphasis on the "right to die" has given suicide and euthanasia a measure of acceptability and respectability. Amazingly there are agencies today which champion the right of individuals to self-destruct as an answer to their crushing physical and psychological problems. The whole debate over the sanctity of human life, assisted suicide and euthanasia is very much in the public domain at present. In my native Northern Ireland with a population of one and a half million people, there is an average of one hundred and thirty-six suicides each year. In recent years there is an alarming escalation of suicides among our young people.

WHAT IS SUICIDE?

In essence suicide is the act of voluntarily and deliberately killing oneself. The word suicide comes from two Latin words, sui, meaning "self," and caedere, meaning "to kill." People who attempt suicide generally experience needs and situations of various sorts and faced with pressing issues for which suicide is perceived to be their best "solution" therefore, they engage in the act of self-murder.

Both the definition and the act of suicide may appear quite simple but the causes and circumstances of the act itself and the consequences that follow are much more complex than is frequently thought. Words frequently associated with the suicidal person are: hopelessness, worthlessness, depression, fear, revenge, protest, release from pain, a cry for help, anger and regret. Often there is a history of low self-esteem, grief, sexual abuse, incest, fear, sexual deviation, drug or alcohol abuse, shame, financial collapse or unemployment and debt, chronic or terminal illness.   Some of these create the obsessive belief that life will never change for the good.   The victim feels cornered to the extent that he or she sees death as the only way out of this bewildered state.

Suicidal tendencies may be the result of chemical imbalance and clinical depression in a person.   There is always the danger in manic depression that it will push the person over the edge.   Such an individual needs medical attention and probably psychiatric treatment and should not be left unattended when they are so depressed.

Some one has said, "Suicide is a permanent answer to temporary problems."   That is not even debatable.   Suicide answers nothing and does not solve any problems.   Our problems are temporary but suicide creates greater problems than any difficulty the victim may try to solve. "To run away from trouble is a form of cowardice," wrote Aristotle.   The sixth commandment forbids murder, we must therefore conclude that suicide is also a sin just as murder is.   The Devil's ultimate ploy is to destroy us and suicide plays into his hand. (John 10:10)

SUICIDE AND THE SCRIPTURES

The Bible is not silent when it comes to suicide.   Seven self-inflicted deaths are recorded in the Scriptures but there is no incident in the Bible where suicide was committed by a godly person.   However, this does not mean that Christians are exempt from the peril of suicide.   Sadly too many Christian friends have finished their lives in this tragic and drastic manner.   Again I stress that self-destruction often is the outcome of deep depression caused by mental or chemical imbalance.

There is no moral motive or justification for these suicidal deaths found in the Scriptures.   The Bible merely records the events as historical facts. However, behind each sad suicide in the Bible, an emotion can be traced and this reflects the same emotions experienced in modern times.   Men like Moses, Elijah and Jonah became so discouraged they wanted to die but they did not attempt to take their own lives.

Except for Judas who betrayed the Saviour for the reward of iniquity and went to his own place,(Acts 1:25) nothing is said of their destiny. Judas, the son of perdition went to perdition, not because he committed suicide but because he didn't truly trust the Lord Jesus Christ.

The first instance of suicide in the Bible is that of Abimelech, the son of Gideon and a Judge in Israel. He was wounded in battle when a woman slung a millstone that hit Abimelech on the head.

Then he called hastily unto the young man his armour bearer, and said unto him, Draw thy sword, and slay me, that men say not of me, A woman slew him. And his young man thrust him through, and he died. And when the men of Israel saw that Abimelech was dead, they departed every man unto his place. (Judges 9:50 -55).

The death of Samson was self-inflicted when he brought down a house upon himself and thereby destroyed the Philistine pagans who had gouged out his eyes.

And Samson took hold of the two middle pillars upon which the house stood, and on which it was borne up, of the one with his right hand, and of the other with his left. And Samson said, Let me die with the Philistines. And he bowed himself with all his might; and the house fell upon the lords, and upon all the people that were therein. So the dead which he slew at his death were more than they which he slew in his life. Judges 16:29,30

I Samuel 31.3-6 gives us an account of the suicidal death of Saul, king of Israel and the self-murder of his armour bearer.

And the battle went sore against Saul, and the archers hit him; and he was sore wounded of the archers. Then said Saul unto his armour bearer, Draw thy sword, and thrust me through therewith; lest these uncircumcised come and thrust me through, and abuse me. But his armour bearer would not; for he was sore afraid. Therefore Saul took a sword, and fell upon it. And when his armour bearer saw that Saul was dead, he fell likewise upon his sword, and died with him. So Saul died, and his three sons, and his armour bearer, and all his men, that same day together."

Like Abimelech, Saul was also wounded in battle and asked his armour bearer to hasten his death. When the soldier refused, Saul drew his own sword and fell on it. The armour bearer followed the king in self-destruction.

When David lamented the death of Saul he only remembered the virtues of the King even though he indulged in gross sin and finally committed suicide. (2 Samuel 1:17-27)

Another suicide in the Scriptures is the death of Ahithophel, advisor to David and Absalom.

And when Ahithophel saw that his counsel was not followed, he saddled his ass, and arose, and gat him home to his house, to his city, and put his household in order, and hanged himself, and died, and was buried in the sepulchre of his father." (2 Samuel 17:23)

The King's counsellor was humiliated because his advice was despised so he saddled his donkey and arose and went to his home where he set his house in order and strangled himself.

The record of a suicide in the Old Testament is that of Zimri, who was king of Israel for seven days. He set fire to the Royal palace, killing himself rather than be captured by his enemies. (1 Kings 16:18)

Perhaps the best-known suicide in the Scriptures is that of Judas, the son of perdition who betrayed the Lord Jesus. His death by hanging is recorded in Matthew 27:2-5 and Acts 1:18,19.

Then Judas, which had betrayed him, when he saw that he was condemned, repented himself, and brought again the thirty pieces of silver to the chief priests and elders, Saying, I have sinned in that I have betrayed the innocent blood. And they said, What is that to us? see thou to that. And he cast down the pieces of silver in the temple, and departed, and went and hanged himself.

His suicide followed his remorse for selling and betraying Jesus Christ for the reward of iniquity.

Elijah and Jonah, two of Israel's greatest prophets, got so depressed that they actually wished to die.(IKings 19:4 Jonah 4:)   The Philippian jailer in Acts 16 was in the process of slaying himself. He was facing shame and execution after an earthquake loosed all his prisoners from their chains and sprung open all the prison doors.

Contributing factors to this attempted suicide are relevant to many such cases. The prison officer saw himself as a failure. He anticipated shame and guilt that his failure would bring on the family. He feared the reaction of the authorities. He was already staring at death because of the dereliction of duty.

It was then that his own prisoner Paul prevented a gory end of the fearful man's life.

And the keeper of the prison awaking out of his sleep, and seeing the prison doors open, he drew out his sword, and would have killed himself, supposing that the prisoners had been fled. But Paul cried with a loud voice, saying, Do thyself no harm: for we are all here. Then he called for a light, and sprang in, and came trembling, and fell down before Paul and Silas, And brought them out, and said, Sirs, what must I do to be saved? And they said, Believe on the Lord Jesus Christ, and thou shalt be saved, and thy house. And they spake unto him the word of the Lord, and to all that were in his house. And he took them the same hour of the night, and washed their stripes; and was baptized, he and all his, straightway.

In all these occurrences, it is important to note that none of the suicides is viewed favourably or viewed as a legitimate option, even in the most difficult of times.

THE MOTIVES FOR SUICIDE

There are no simple nor single answers to why people commit suicide. It is a complex act which presents perplexing questions. In his book, Why Suicide, Eric Marcus, whose father committed suicide, wrote out of painful experience.

The suicide of a loved one leaves in its wake a painful confusion that is expressed with a one-word question: Why? Embedded in that question are three others that begin with why: why didn't we see it coming? Why didn't he/she come to us for help. Above all else, why did he/she do it?

Anyone who has lost a friend or loved one to suicide has grappled with all these questions and there are no easy answers.

In the excellent booklet "Basic Questions on Suicide and Euthanasia" (Kregel – Bio Basic Series) the authors state,

> "What are some of the emotional trip wires or triggers that precipitate suicide? They are varied and are seldom solitary events or feelings. Often they are a series of unresolved events and feelings that eventually become too great of a burden to carry alone. Among them are depression, alcoholism, substance abuse, anger, revenge, illness, physical infirmity, loss of a loved one, loss of a close friend, loss of a job or other financial setback, public humiliation or loss of social status, and schizophrenia or personality disorders. For each of these triggers, or a combination of them, there is an apparent and ever-growing inability to alleviate (lessen) the emotional pain. In such cases, suicide seems to be the only means of relief or escape. Suicide is mistakenly seen as a permanent solution to what appears to be an unreasonable personal problem or series of problems. Regrettably, those who choose suicide are either unwilling or unable to see the horrible consequences of their act in the lives of their families and friends. Suicide always creates more pain than it alleviates."

I think it is true to say that for most emotionally-disturbed people who finally go to this extreme they are not really wanting to die. I have found it to be more the case that they want to find a way out of their problems and trouble. Suicide is not about the problem of dying. It is more the result of problems encountered in life. Suicidal people feel they have exhausted all the possible options and without any other escape from their oppressive feelings they opt for death as the only way out.

The root cause of this feeling may be deep and probably of long duration. As a Christian I recognise that not all the problems that a suicidal person faces are spiritual. As I have already stressed suicide may follow as a result of chemical imbalance and clinical depression. However, the ultimate root of every problem is spiritual. When the Philippian jailer pulled the sword to end his life and solve his dilemma of shame and guilt Paul not only prevented suicide but led the man to salvation in Jesus Christ.

There are two main goals that we should keep before us when trying to help suicidal people. The first is to tactfully apply the Scriptures as the only form of hope. We should also look out for the practical welfare of the person.

COPING WITH THE CRISIS AND FALL OUT

Suicide has a devastating impact on families and friends of the victim. The emotions that follow the aftermath of a suicide range from shock, anger, grief, fear, guilt, depression, shame, denial, self-recrimination, and confusion. Those who want to help the close friends of the deceased feel totally inadequate when confronted with this challenge.

Observe some principles from the Apostle Paul's action to prevent the death of the jailer.

i. Paul listened to the cry for help from the jailer who was at the point of suicide. Listening to people is a very important ministry. Often the despairing person will use vocabulary that indicates they have given up hope. Suicide seldom happens unannounced. Such cries as "I can't take any more." Or "I don't see any way out." Often reveal the depth of the victim's hopelessness.

ii. Paul looked at the plight of the man. Did he see the glint of the sword in the night? Did he notice the look of despair from his captor? Paul undoubtedly saw the man needed help. To help the distraught person we should watch for their actions and attitudes — the withdrawal from company. Often there are tell-tale signs in the victim's conversation or action.

iii. Paul was available to help and encourage the person. Paul did not come up with an easy solution to the jailer's dilemma. There are no easy solutions. In Paul's interaction with the man he did not judge him, or show anger toward him. Neither did he seek to provoke guilt or tell him to "snap out of it." Tact and patience were required. We must not minimize the depth of the person's despair and be prepared to encourage and help. Paul perceived immediately the depth of the jailer's despair and offered hope in Jesus Christ. The answer to guilt is forgiveness through Jesus Christ. The assurance of God's love and the practical friendship and fellowship which Paul demonstrated with the family are principles that we must employ in seeking to help those who are suicidal.

iv. Paul befriended the man and his family and cultivated a relationship. Despair and shame need to be replaced by hope and the assurance that there is a future for the person. Hope is the vital factor. Proverbs 13:12 indicates the importance of hope, "Hope deferred maketh the heart sick: but when the desire cometh, it is a tree of life."

Offer genuine friendship to the depressed and despairing person. A British publication once offered a prize for the best definition of a friend. Among the thousands of answers received was the following: "One who multiplies joys, divides grief, and whose honesty is inviolable." The winning definition read: "A friend is the one who comes in when the whole world has gone out."

After a suicide there follows the inevitable sense of guilt and blame from those nearest the deceased. These all become victims because of the tragedy. We need to help them recover and readjust to life without the one they lost. They might well express what the Psalmist felt in Psalm 69:20 "Reproach hath broken my heart ; and I am full of heaviness: and I looked for some to take pity, but there was none; and for comforters, but I found none." It is important that in the midst of their tears and grief they be assured there is hope and that God really cares for them.

Jesus Christ was sent to "bind up the brokenhearted." King David wrote, "The righteous cry, and the LORD heareth, and delivereth them out of all their troubles. The LORD is nigh unto them that are of a broken heart; and saveth such as be of a contrite spirit. Many are the afflictions of the righteous: but the LORD delivereth him out of them all."

The Scriptures which were written for our comfort, bring to all who suffer from broken hearts the promise and assurance that God knows all about our grief, He loves us whatever our tragedies might be and He gives us hope for future days. No matter how deep and dark the valley He has promised to bring us through. He not only cares for us but he is also the One who is touched with every feeling of our infirmity and knows exactly what we need.

Lieutenant Jacquie Pound of Nottinghill Salvation Army Corps, was tragically bereaved when her husband committed suicide. Speaking on BBC's programme "Songs of Praise" she confessed that her husband's unexpected and unexplained death brought a horrendous time of sorrow and deep hurt on the whole family by the one they all loved the most. Jacquie said, "The Lord spoke to me and said 'If you don't forgive him it will ruin your life. If you can forgive the person who has hurt you deeply then God can use it.' I trusted the Lord and said, 'You will have to help me to forgive.' He did and praise the Lord he has helped me to help others."

Jacquie Pounds today has dedicated her life to bring comfort to others who pass through deep times of sorrow.